N W

S

Bob
4:07pm, 18 May 2020

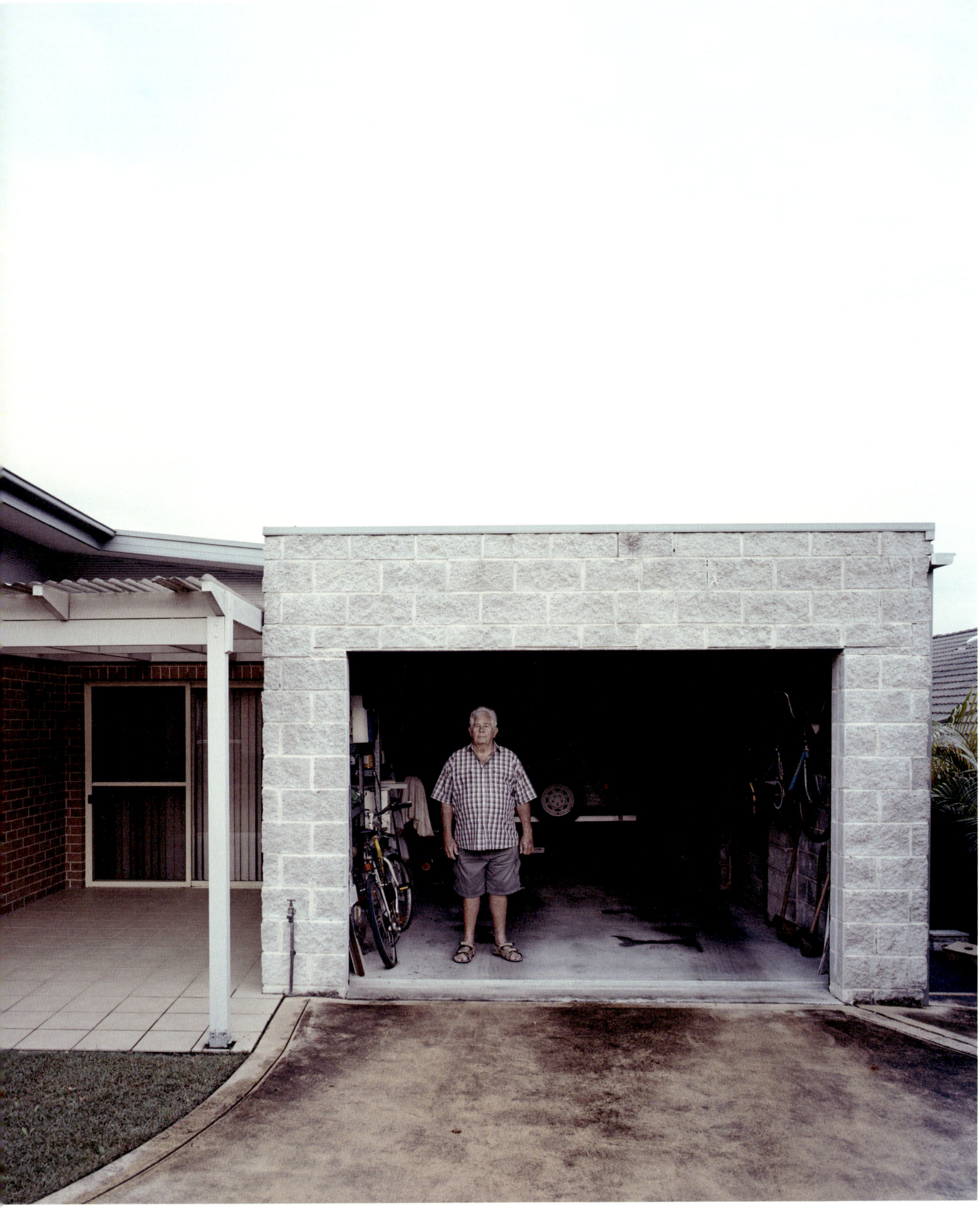

Bonnie, Ren and Ellie
3:32pm, 4 May 2020

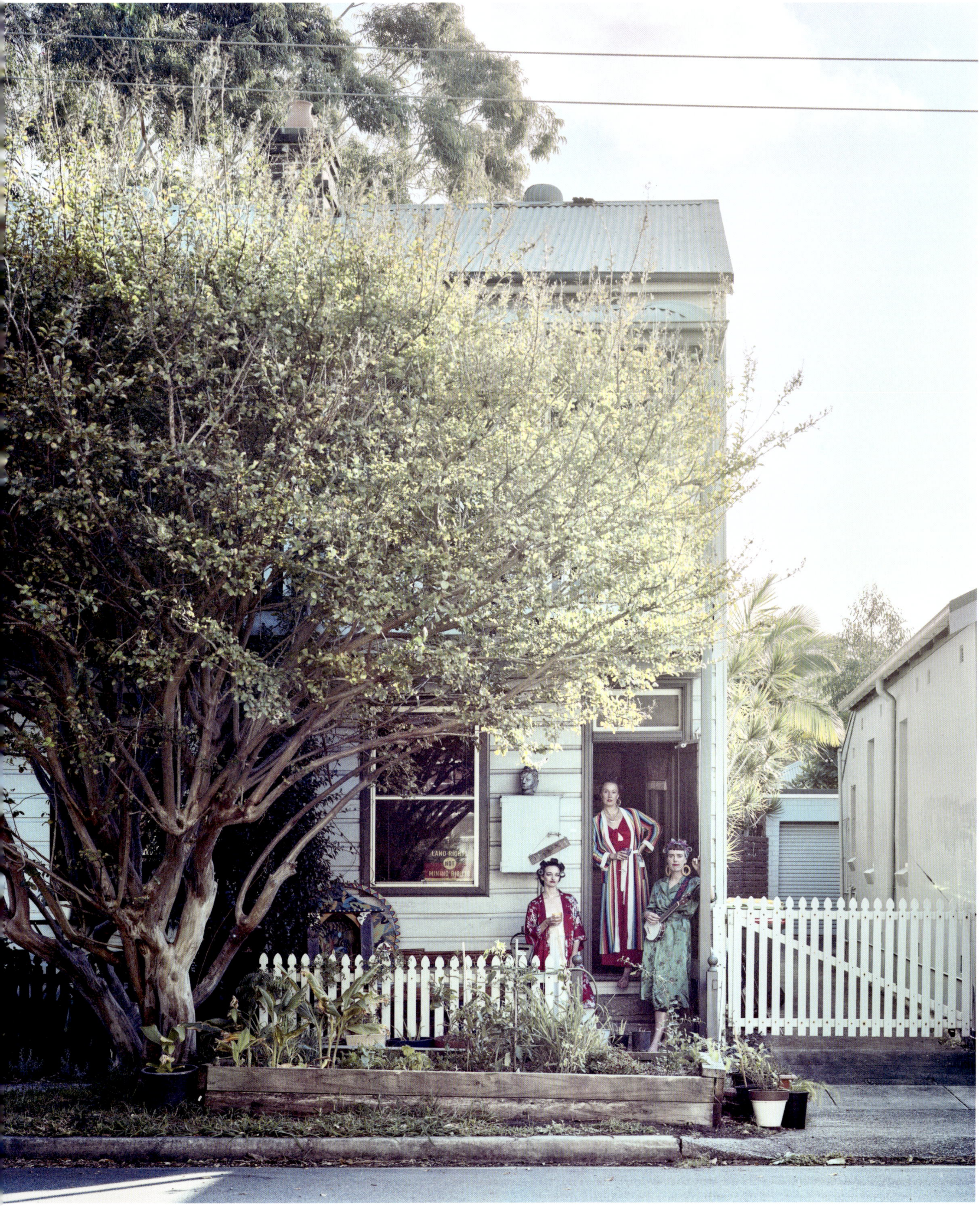
LAND
NOT
MINING

Mel, Henry and Floss
4:47pm, 4 May 2020

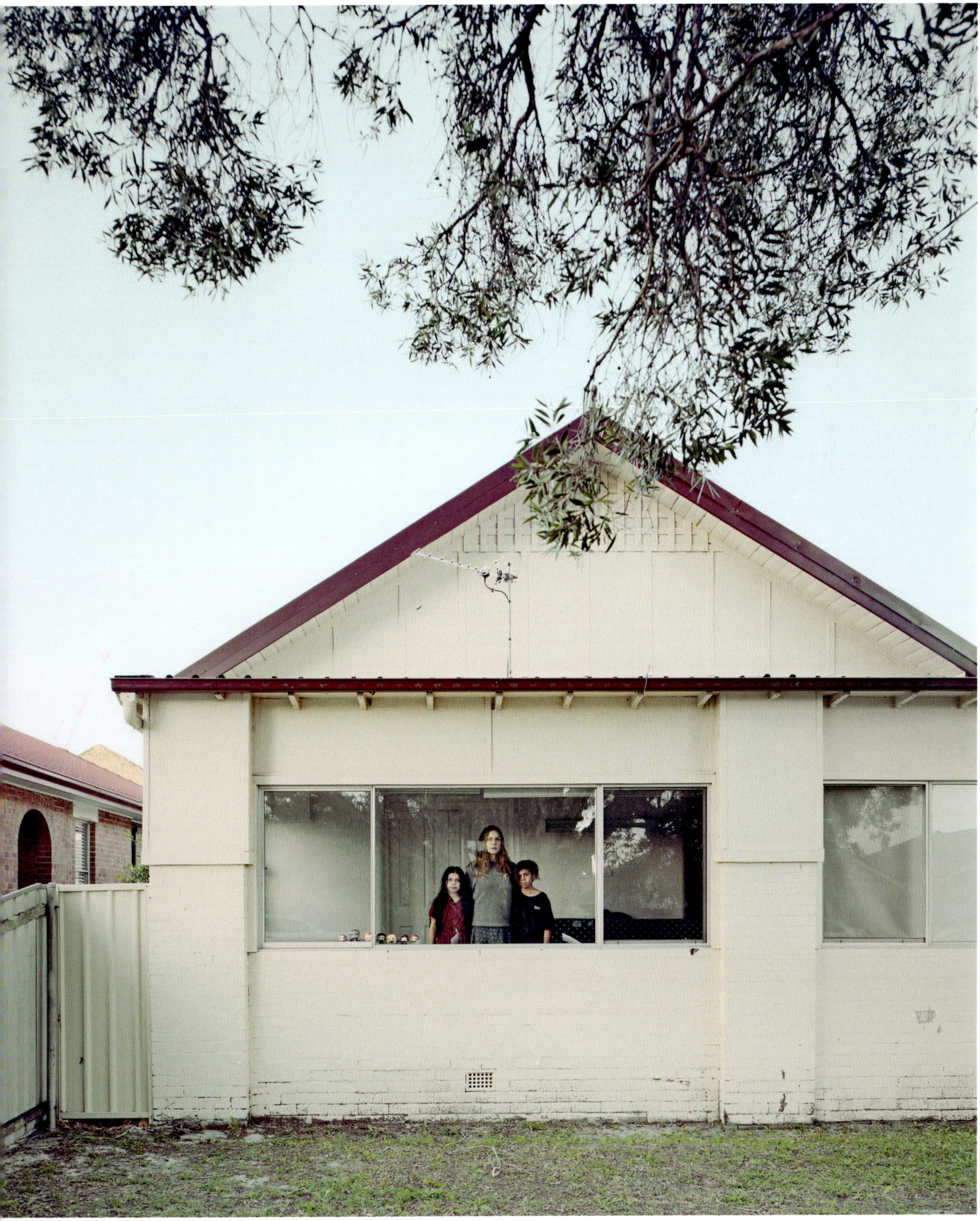

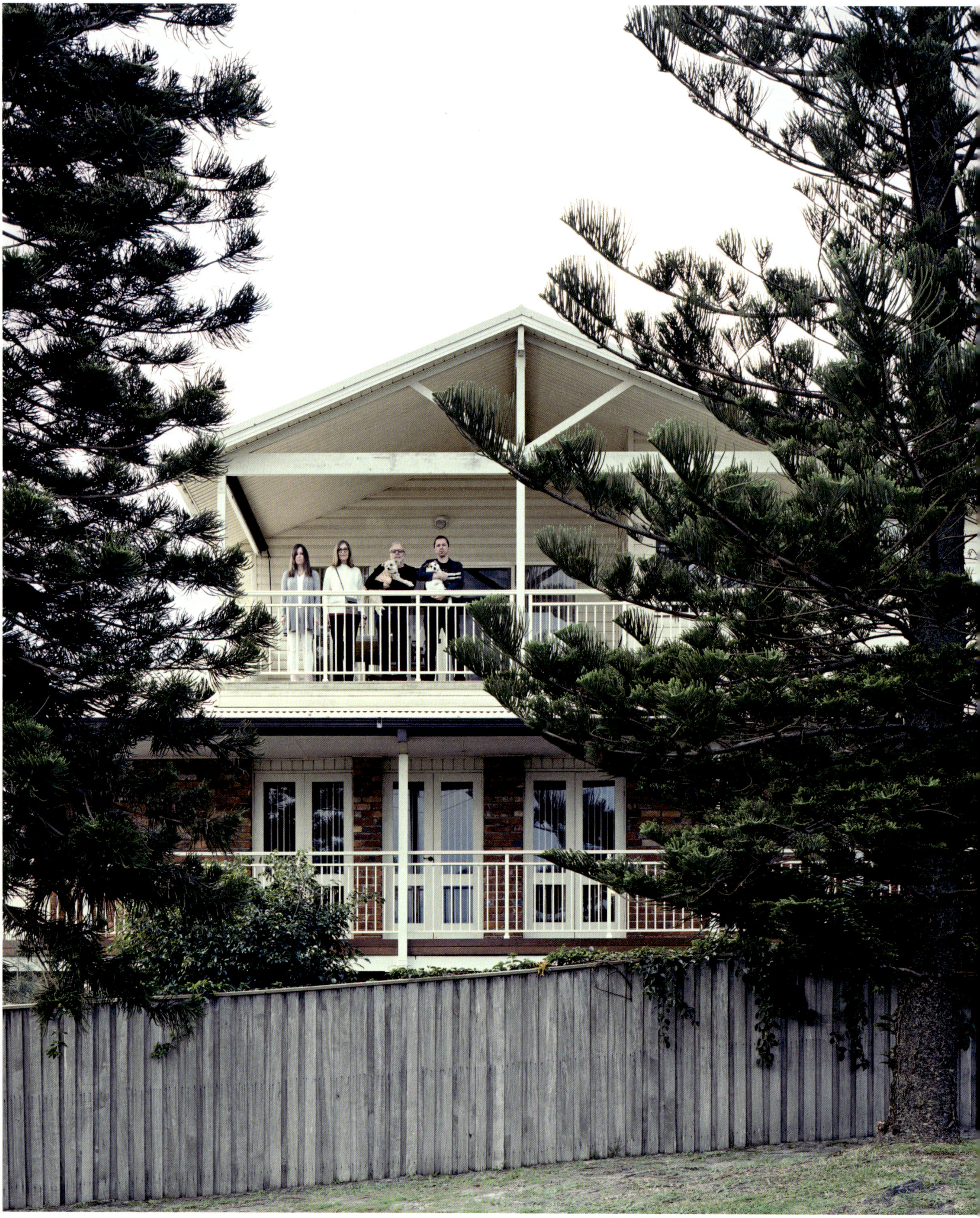

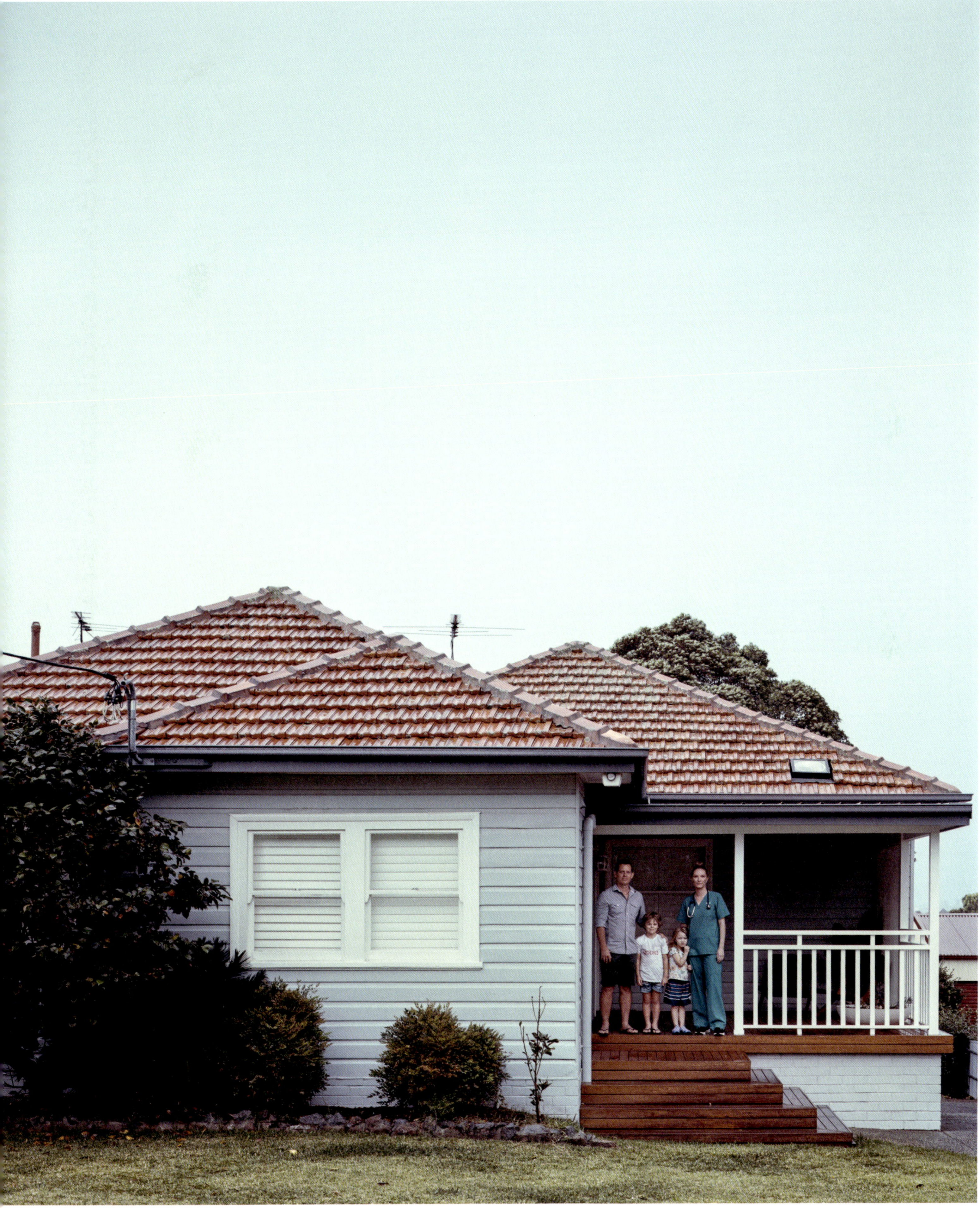

PREVIOUS LEFT
Mike, Liz, Rob and Sarah
3:46pm, 12 June 2020

PREVIOUS RIGHT
Lauren, Greg, Lauchlan and Chloe
4:26pm, 30 April 2020

Juliana, Ben and Eddy
3:26pm, 24 April 2020

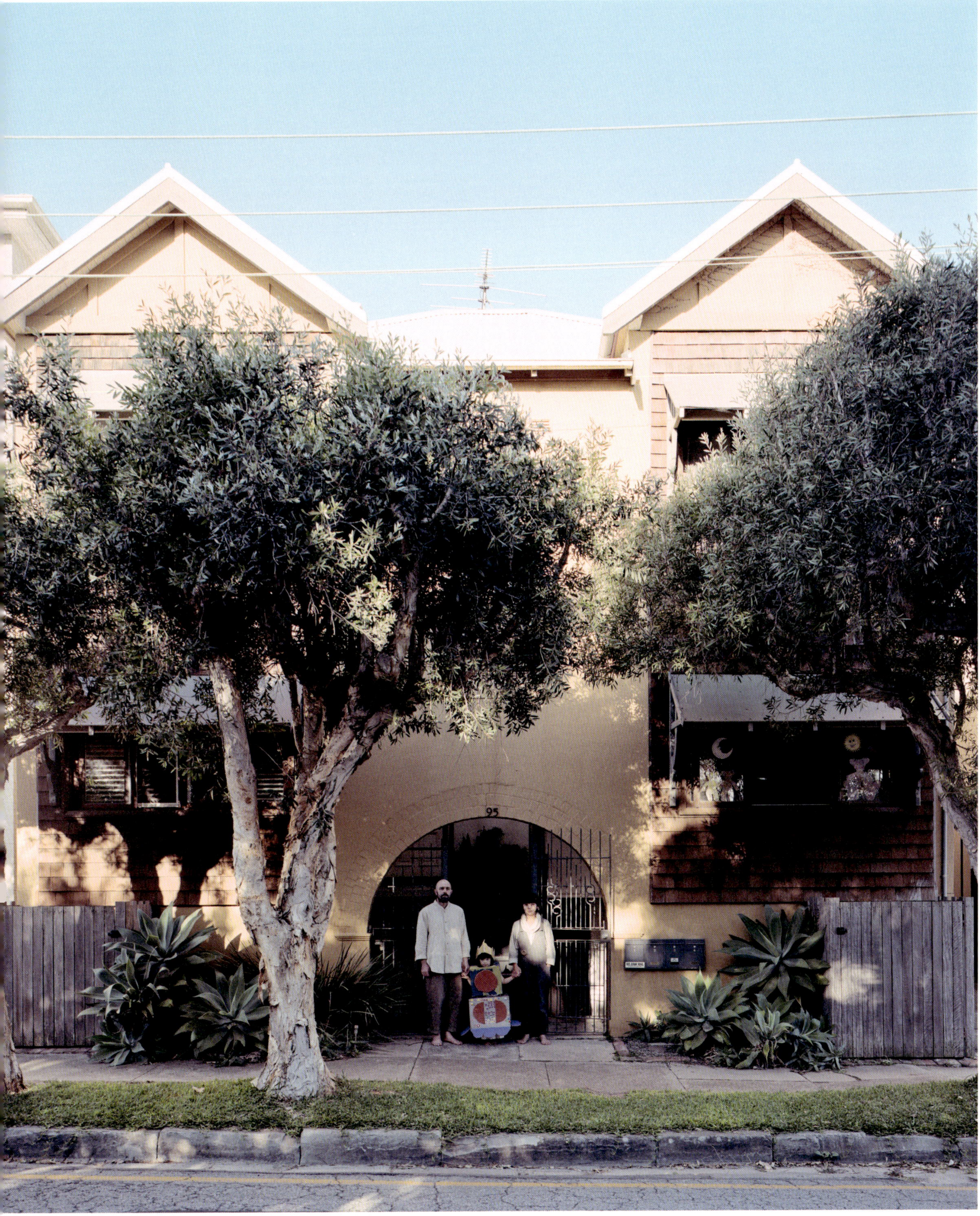
95

Gillean, Kent and Julia
4:28pm, 23 April 2020

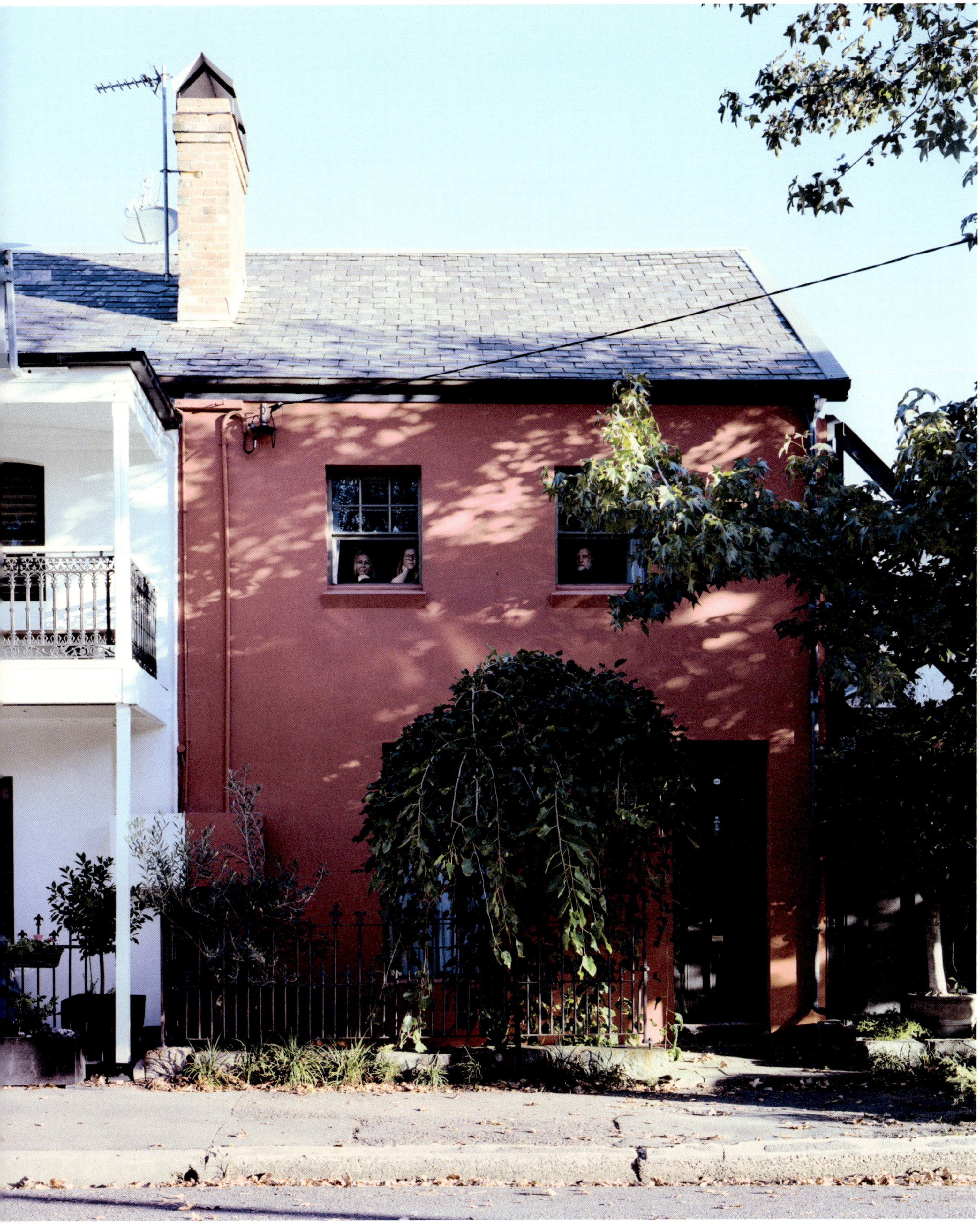

Peter, Sally, Ace and Frankie
4:33pm, 27 May 2020

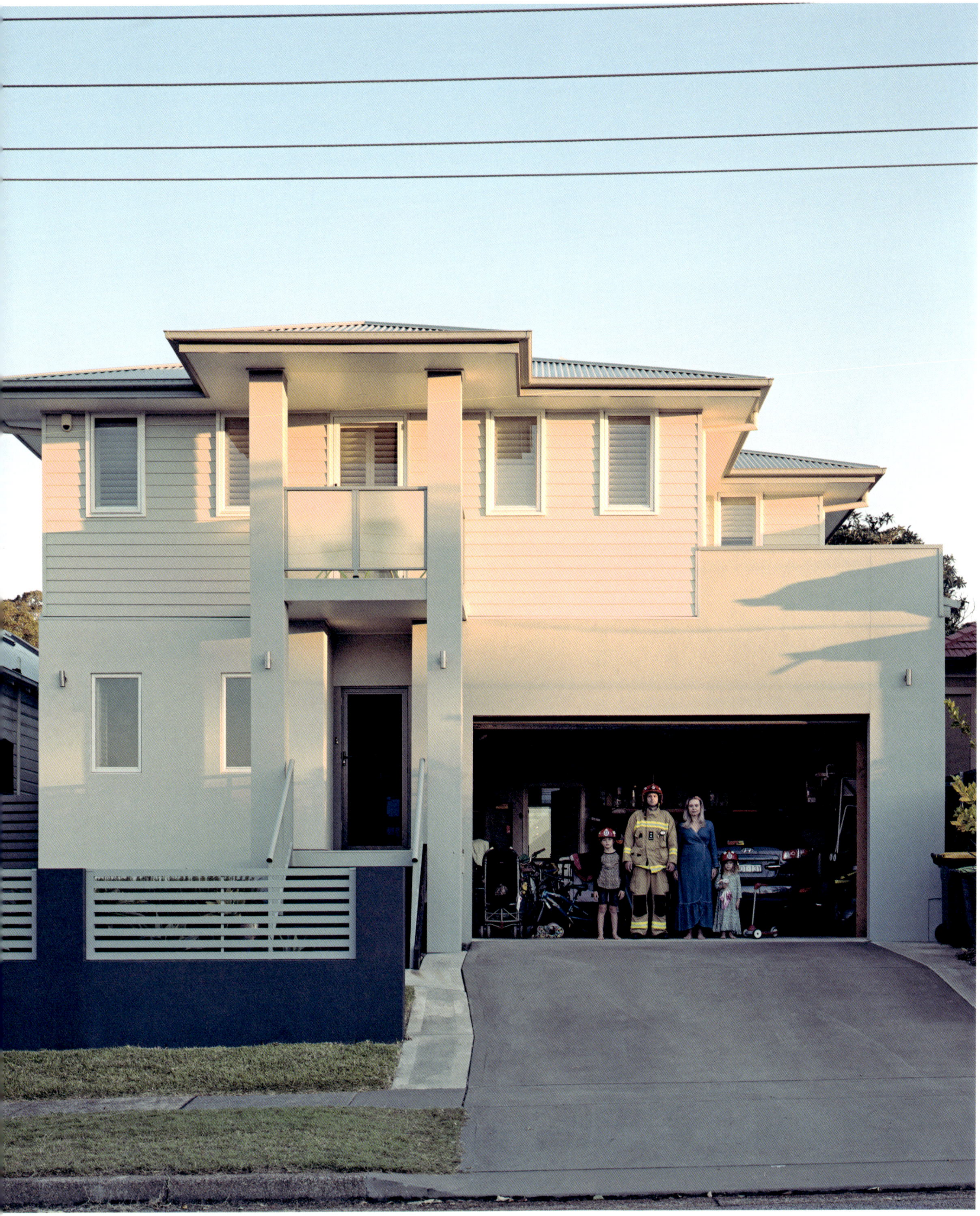

LUKE DAVID KELLETT

N E W
C A S
T L E

GOST

Rod, Tanya, Cooper, Jackson
and Maddie
4:43pm, 6 May 2020

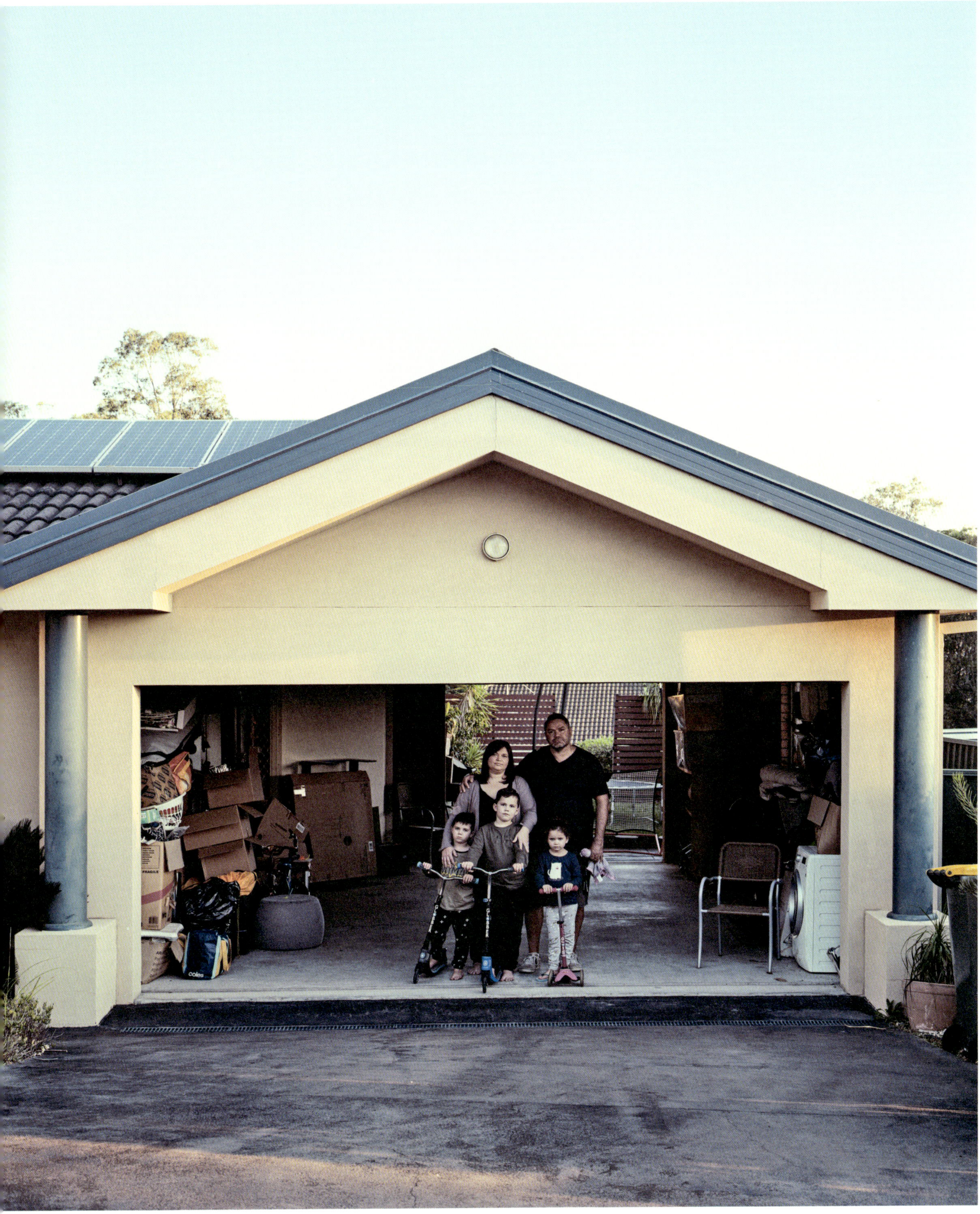
FRAGILE
coles

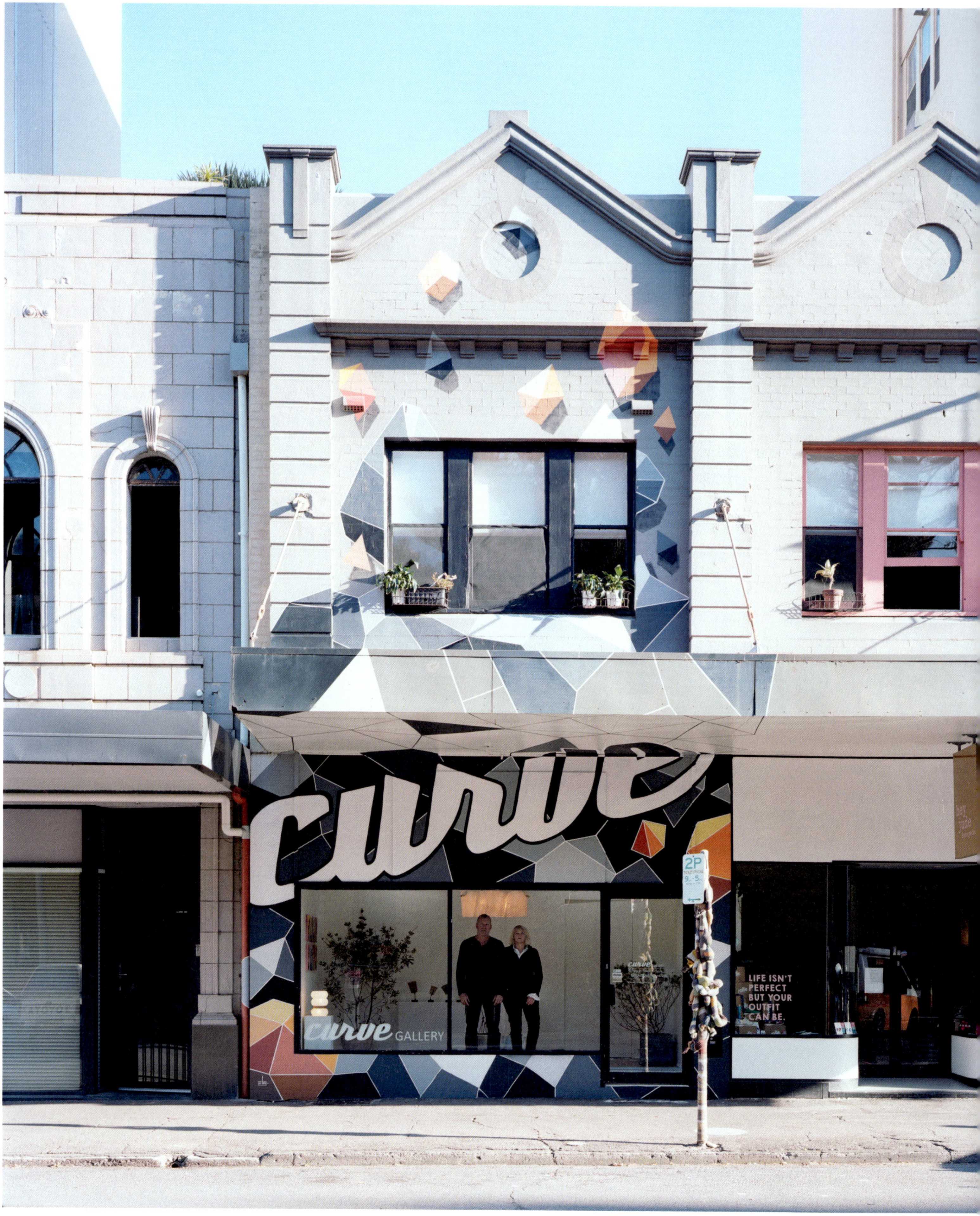
curve
curve GALLERY
LIFE ISN'T PERFECT BUT YOUR OUTFIT CAN BE.
2P

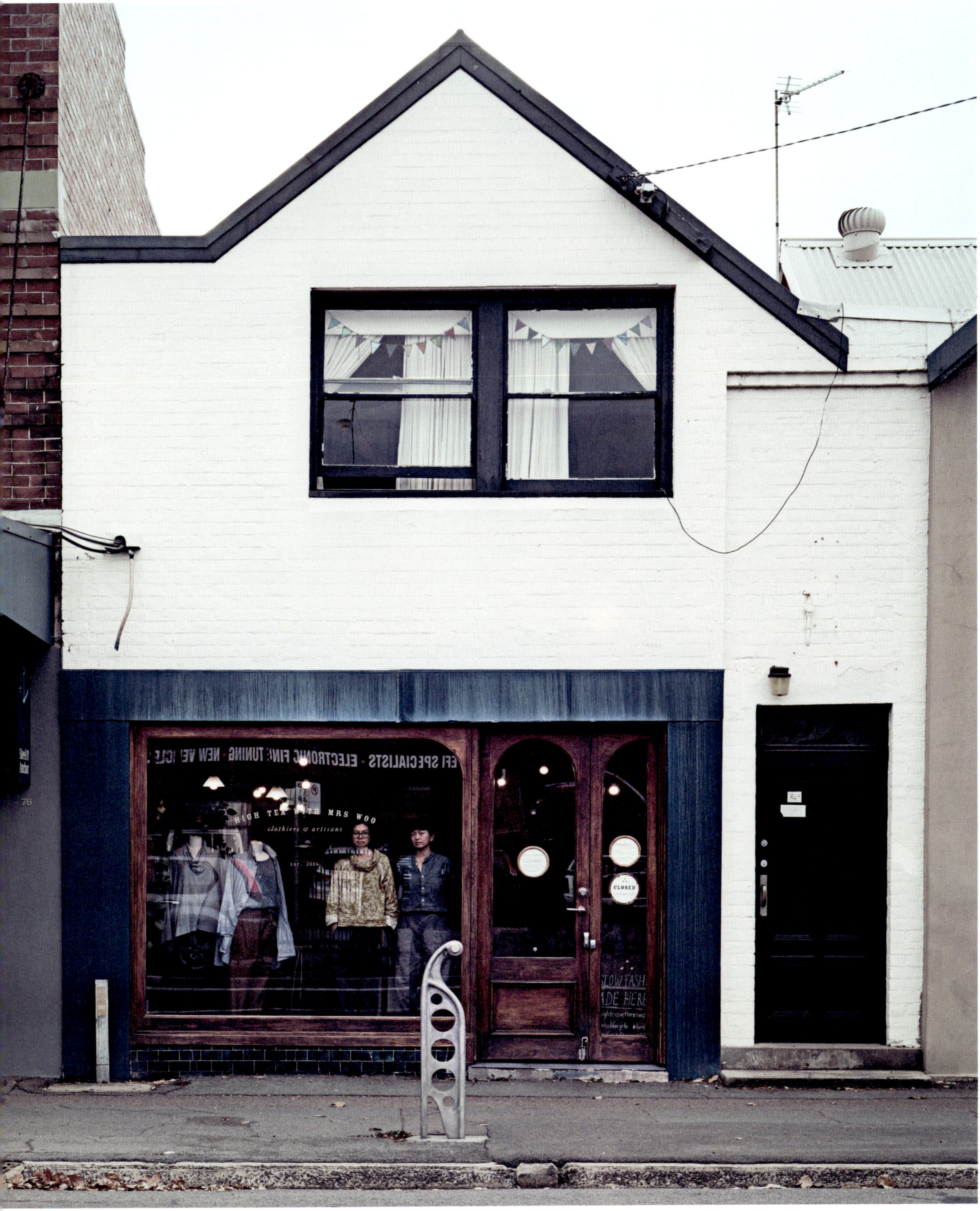
HIGH TEA WITH MRS WOO
clothiers & artisans
CLOSED
76

PREVIOUS LEFT
Lisa and Wayne
3:43pm, 20 August 2021

PREVIOUS RIGHT
Rowena and Angela
4:43pm, 6 May 2020

Kevin and Jean
5:19pm, 5 October 2021

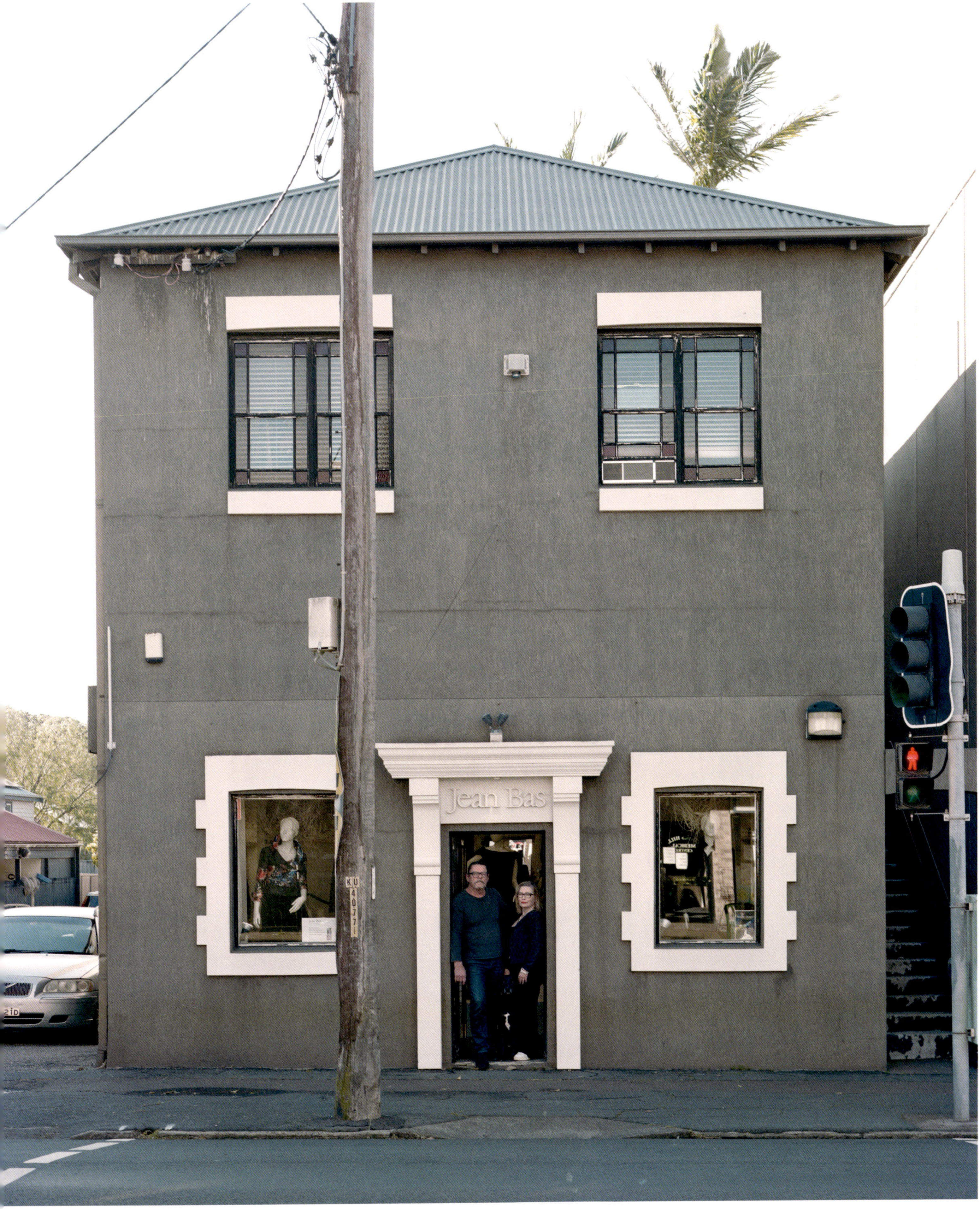
Jean Bas

Luke and Megan
5:58pm, 5 October 2021

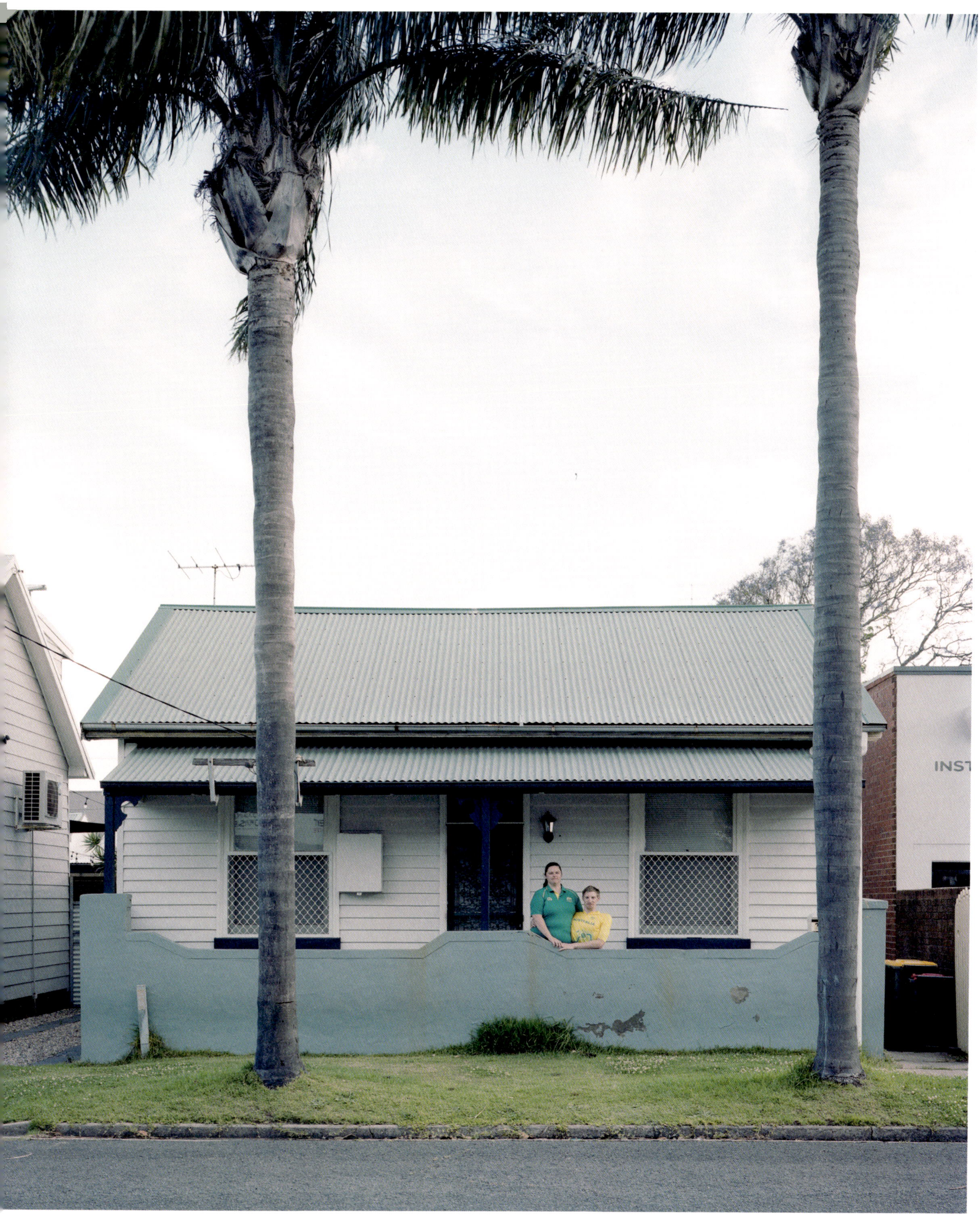
INST

Simone, Ralph and Tino
6:28pm, 9 October 2021

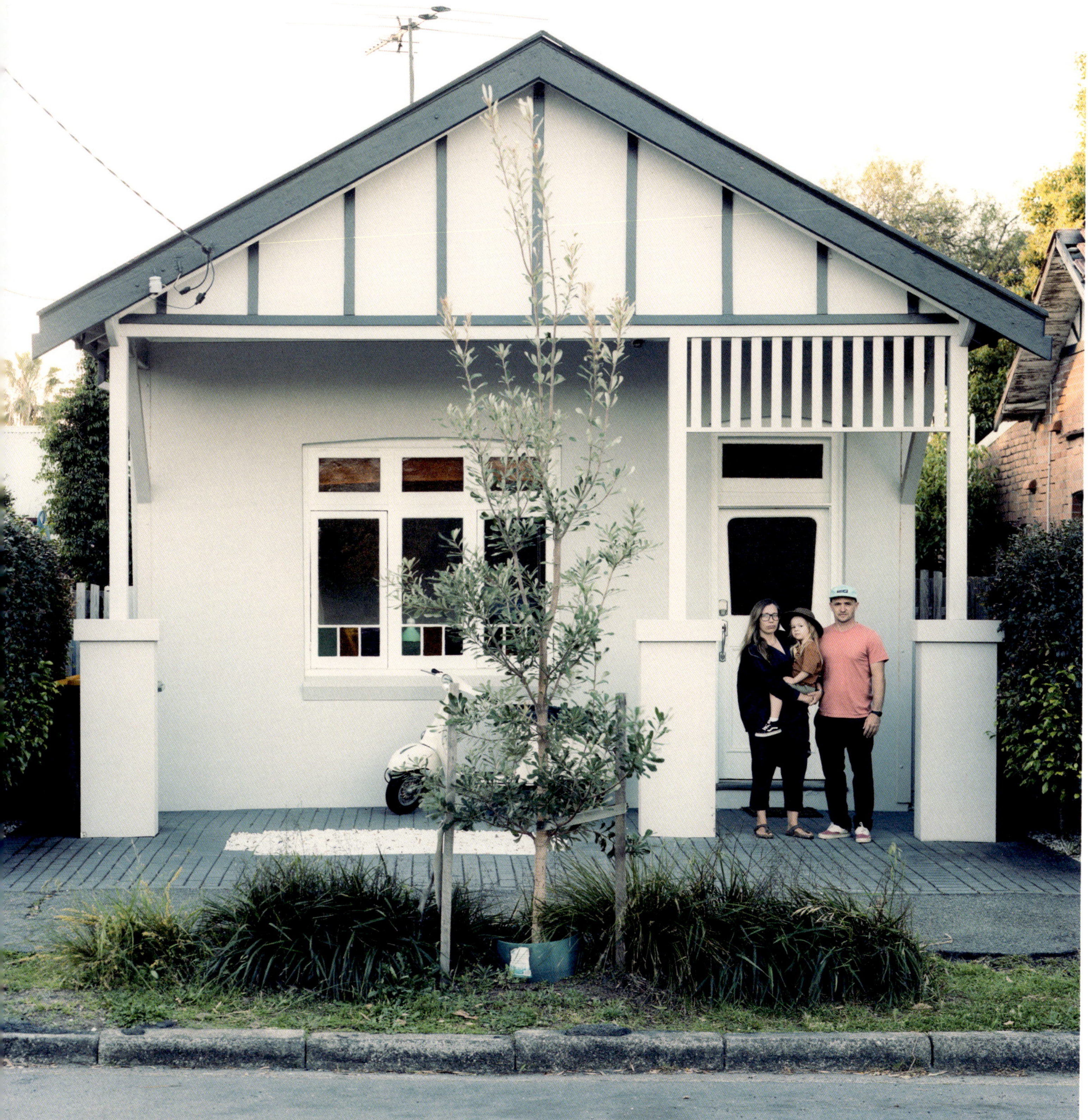

Alex, Alex, Ari, Coan and Eli
2:55pm, 24 April 2020

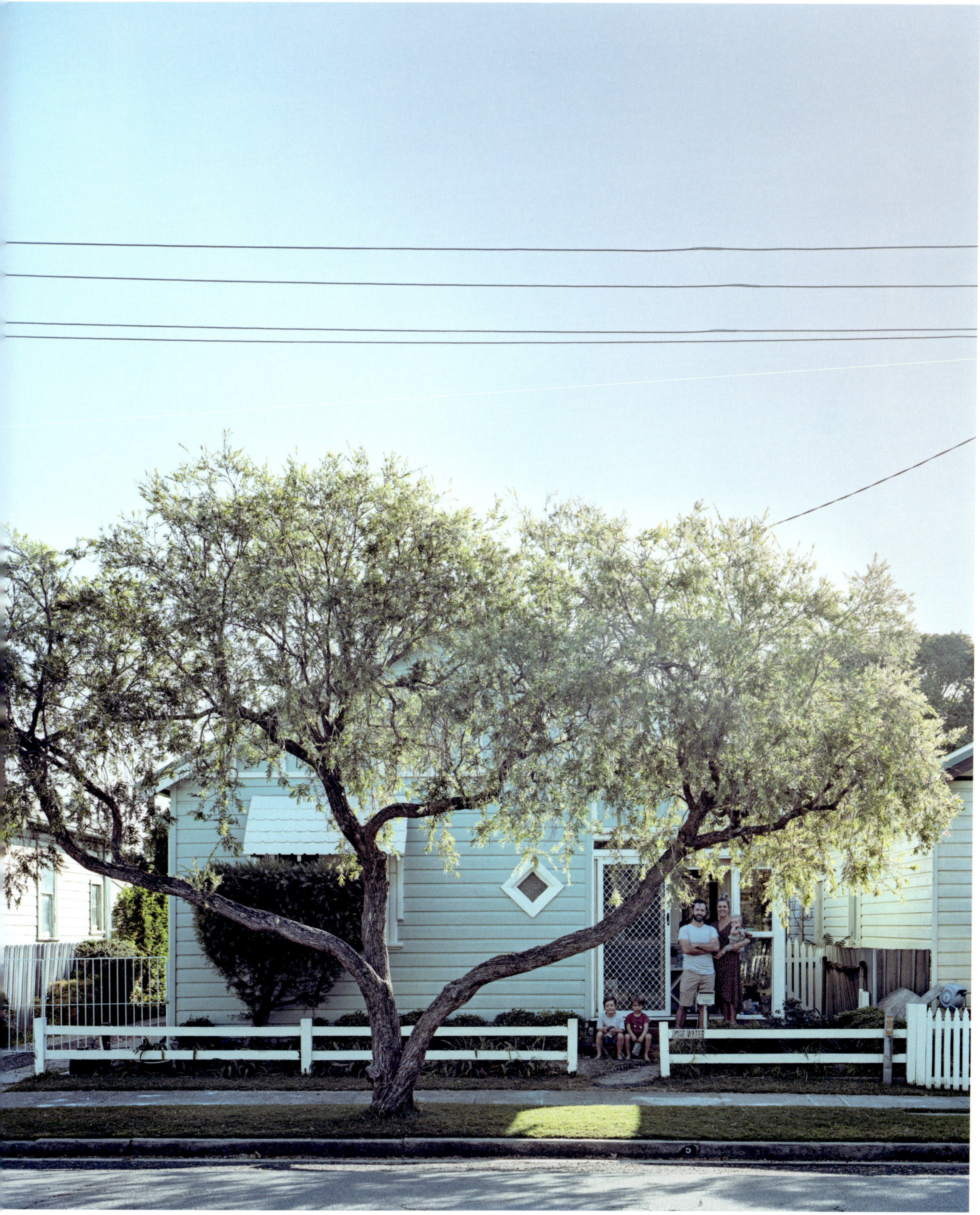

Tracey
5:21pm, 8 October 2021

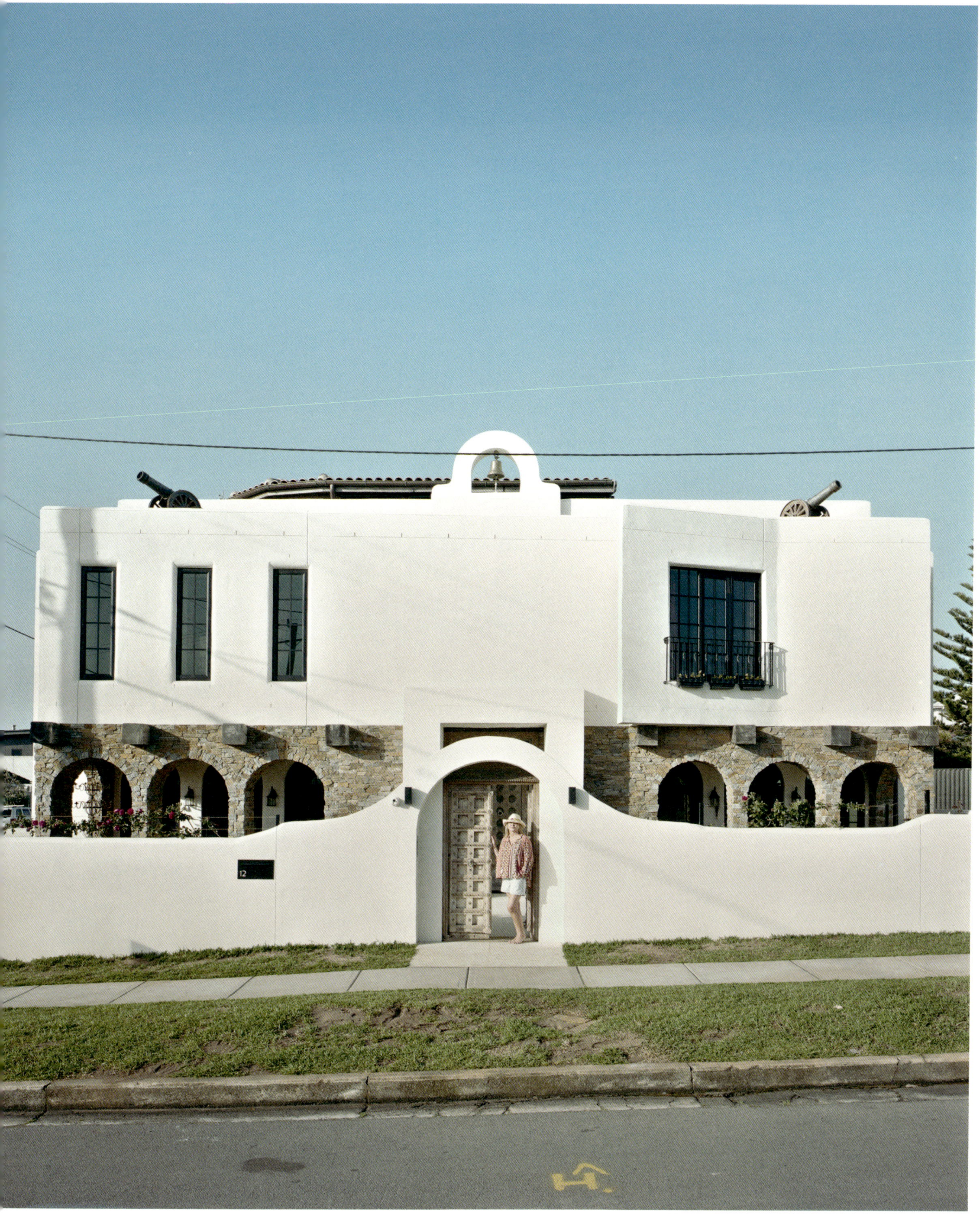
12

Carole and Stan
5:40pm, 7 October 2021

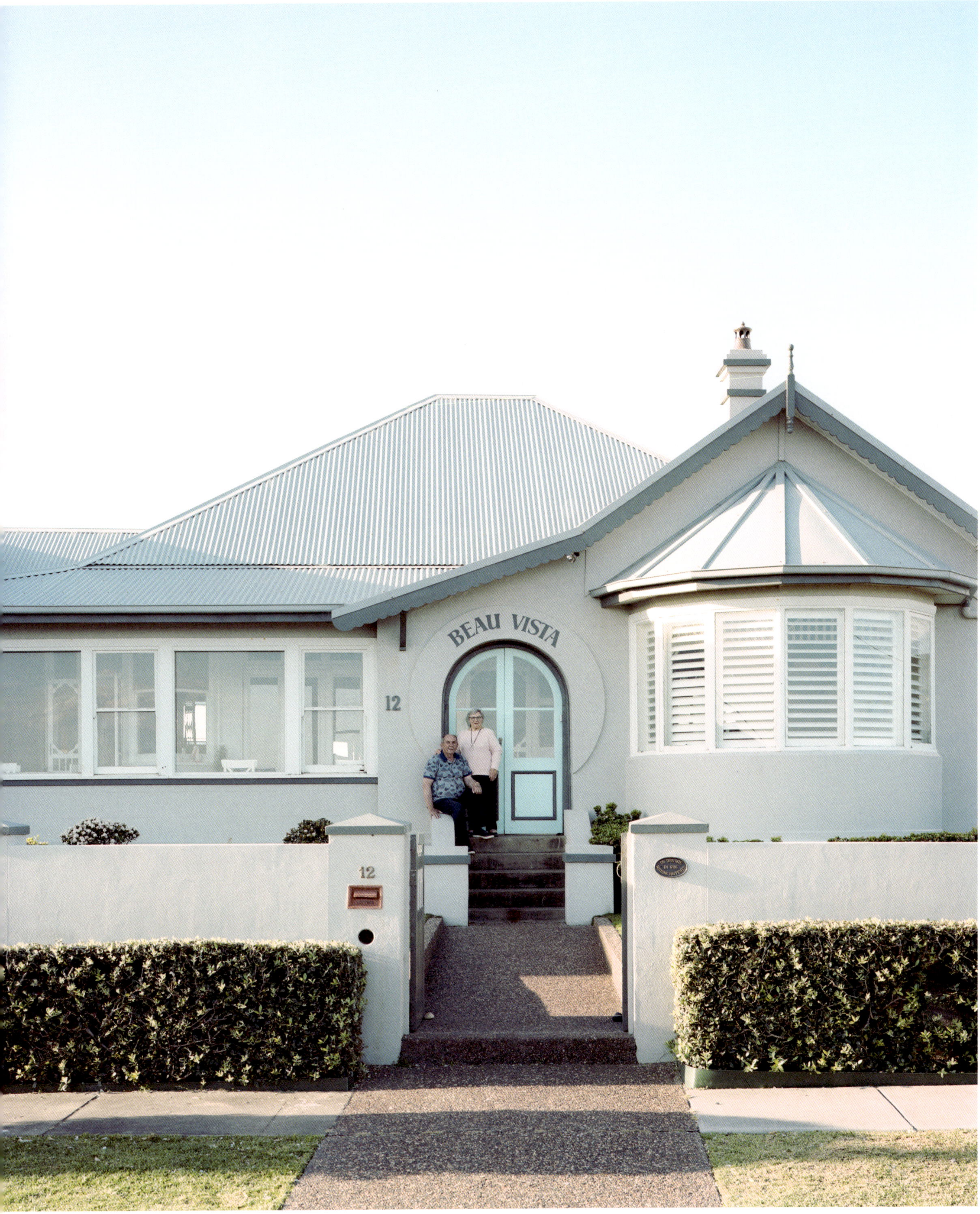
BEAU VISTA
12
12

Abbey
4:48pm, 23 August 2021

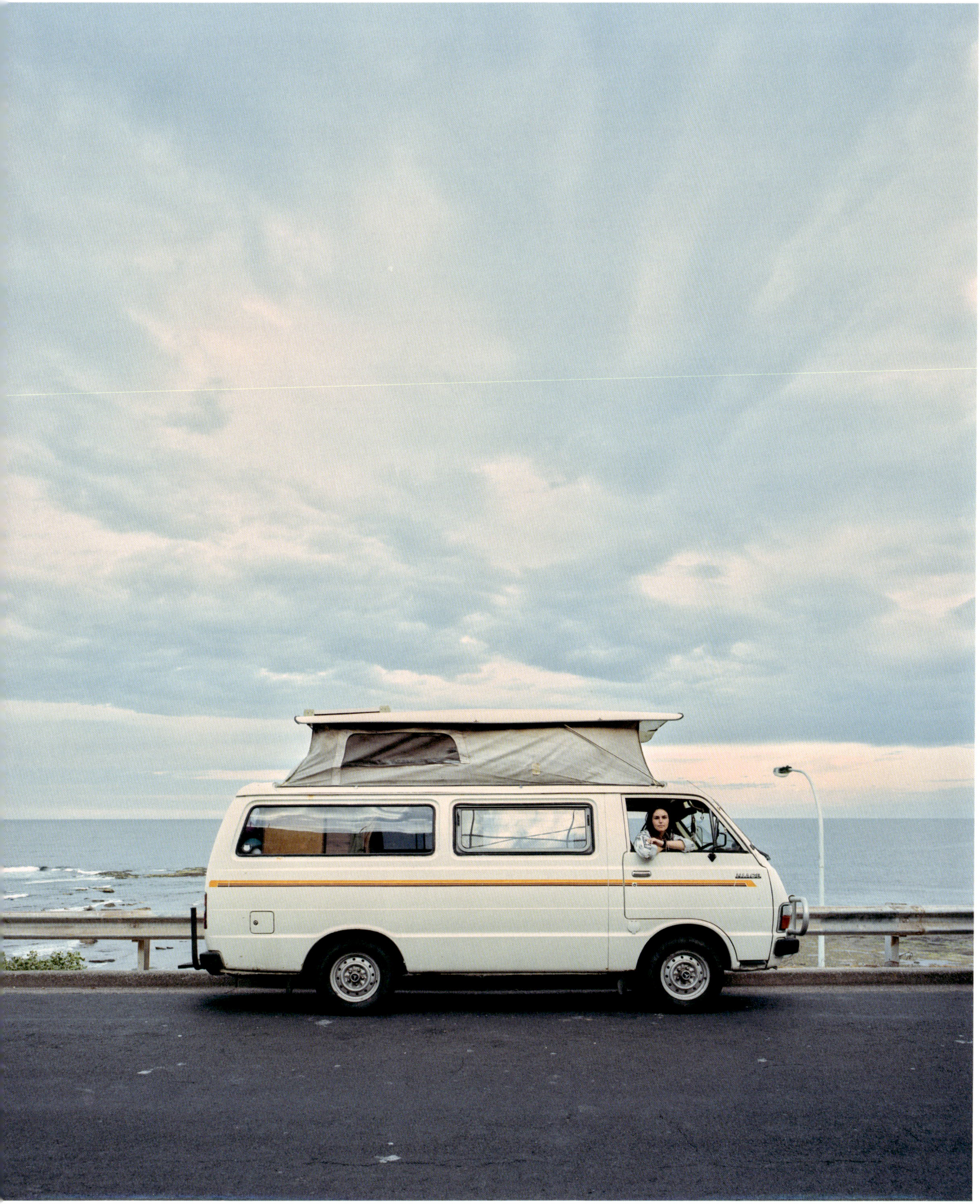

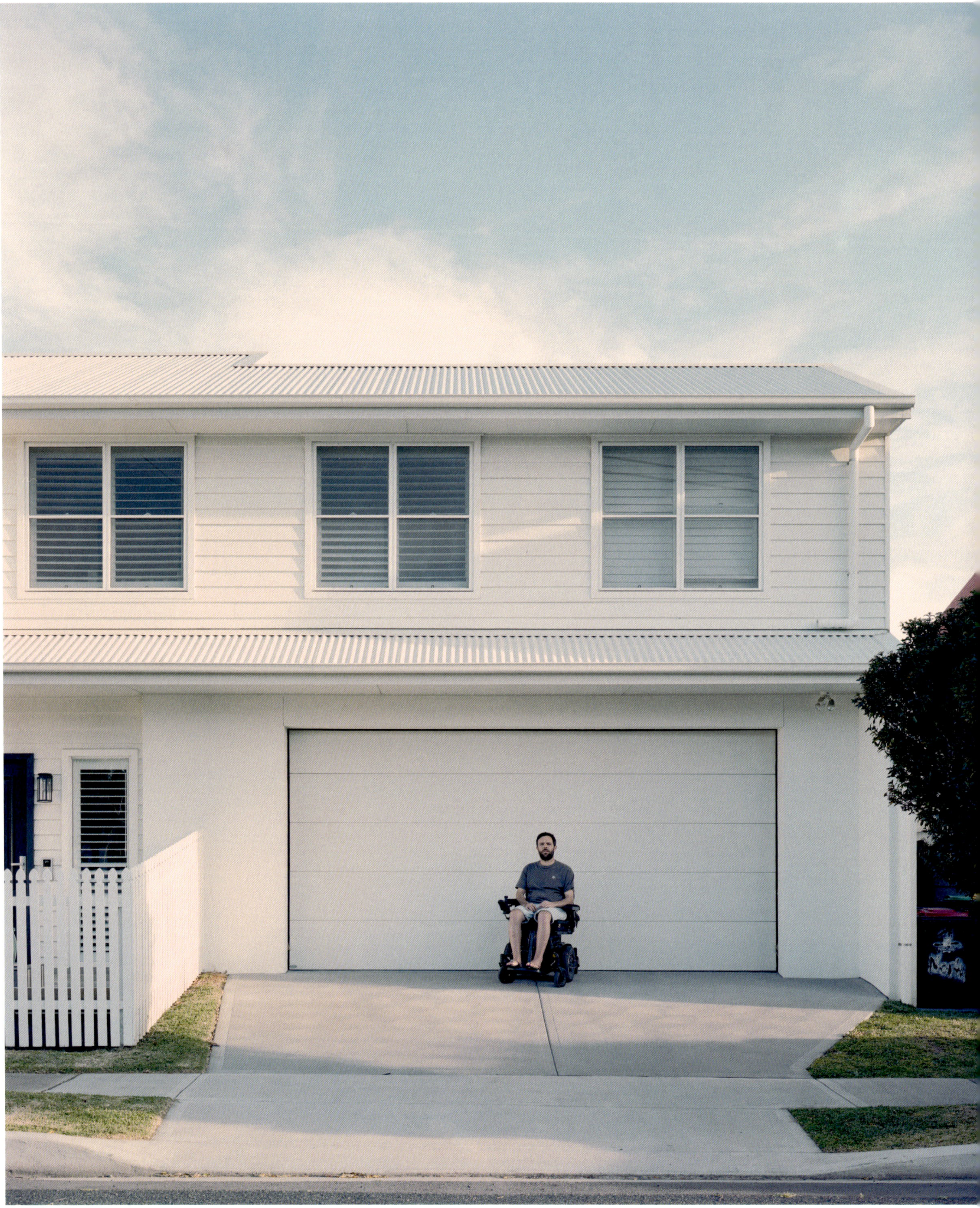

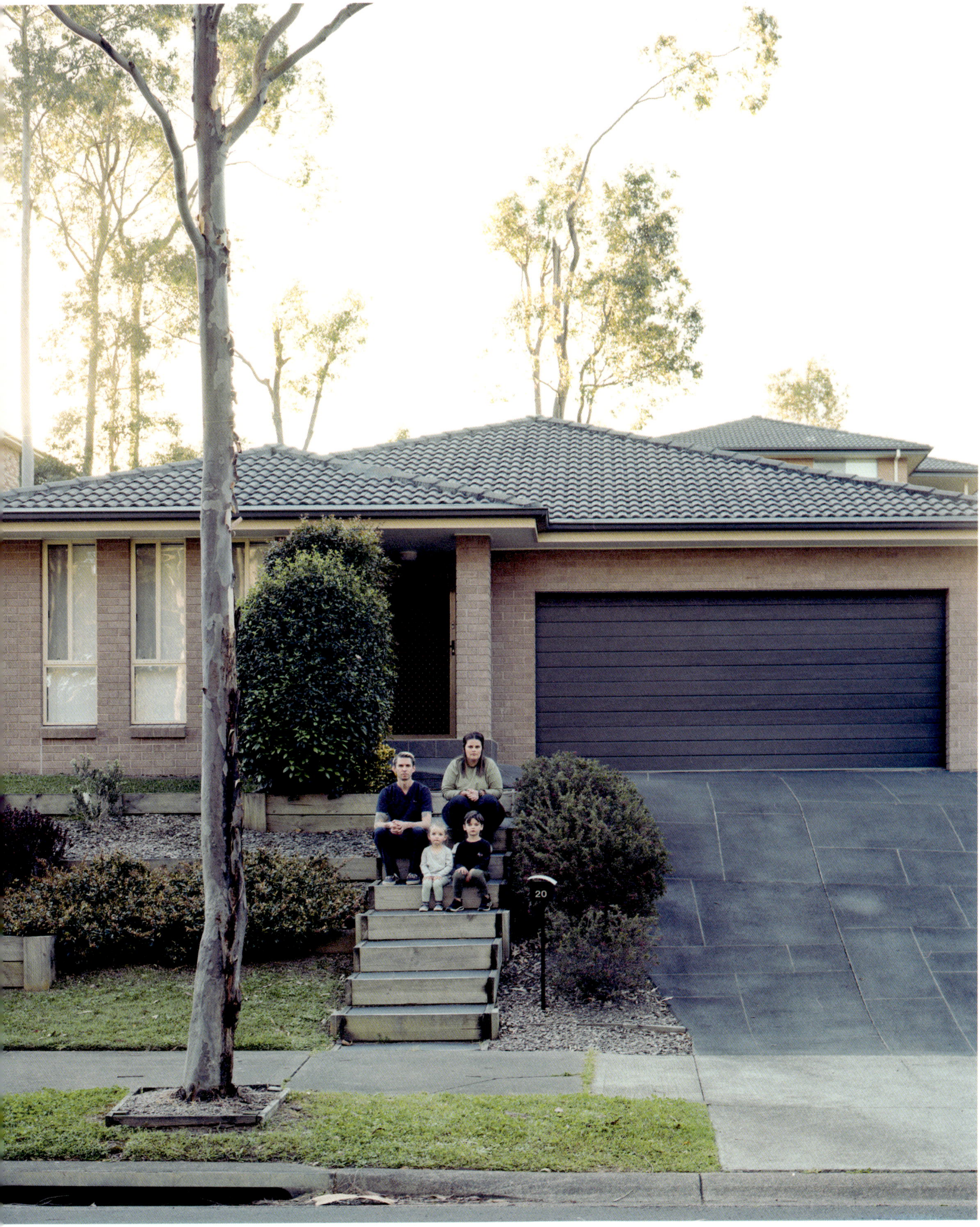
20

PREVIOUS LEFT
Dom
4:27pm, 9 September 2021

PREVIOUS RIGHT
Evan, Hannah and their children
4:47pm, 22 September 2021

Tyler, Luisa, Chloe, Eli, Orchid,
Aidan and Jordan
4:55pm, 13 September 2021

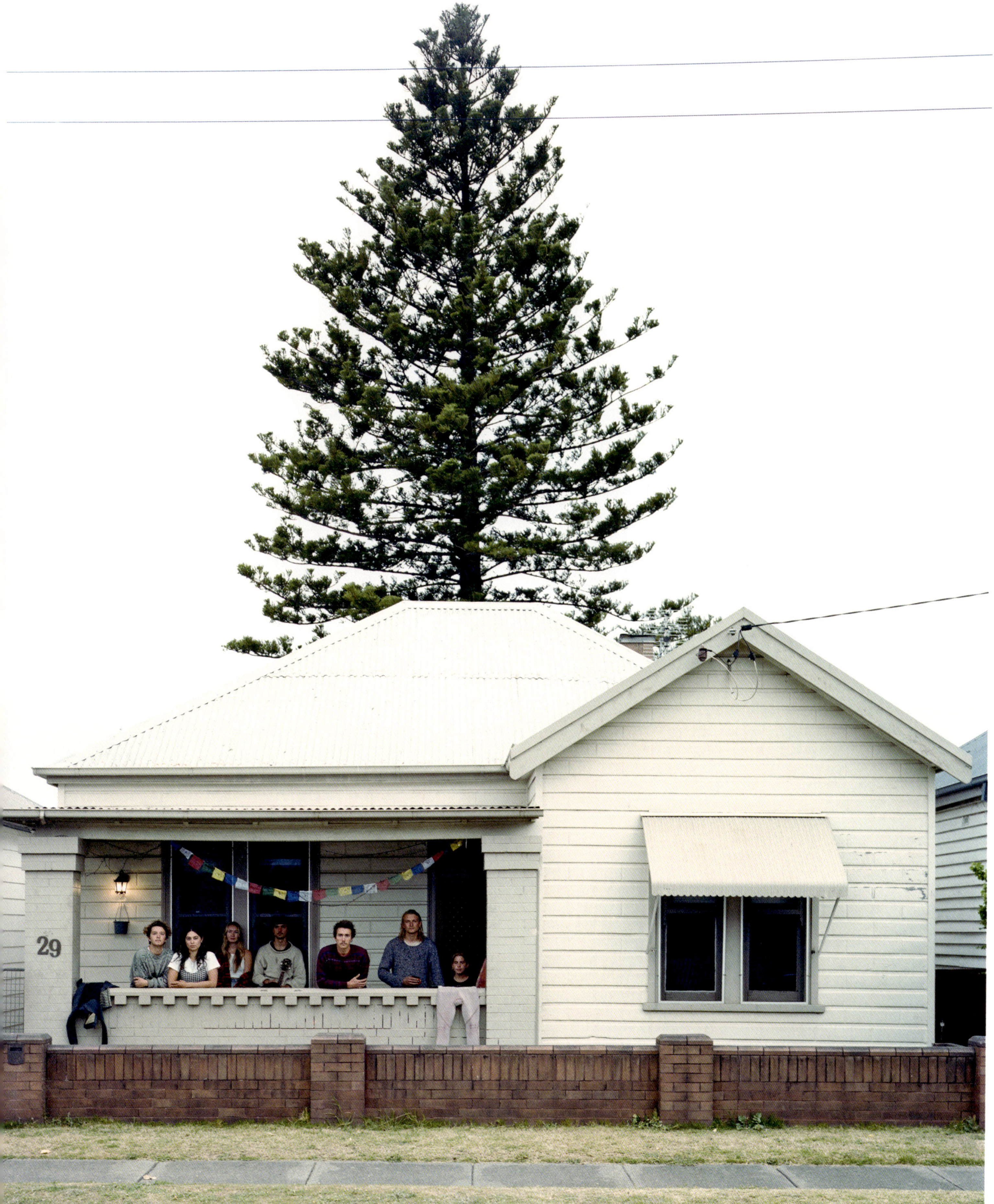
29

Roland, Dave and Stella
4:45pm, 1 May 2020

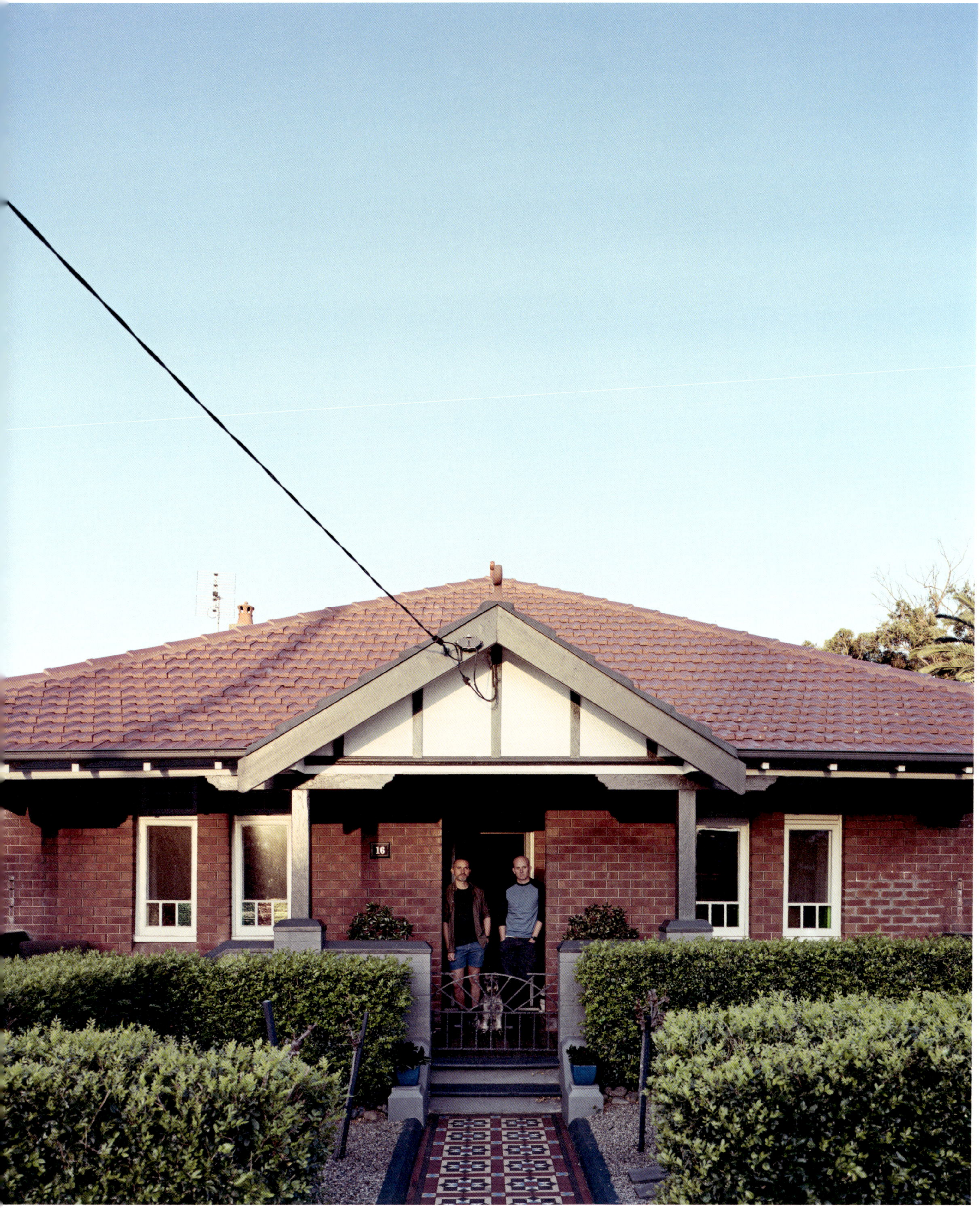
16

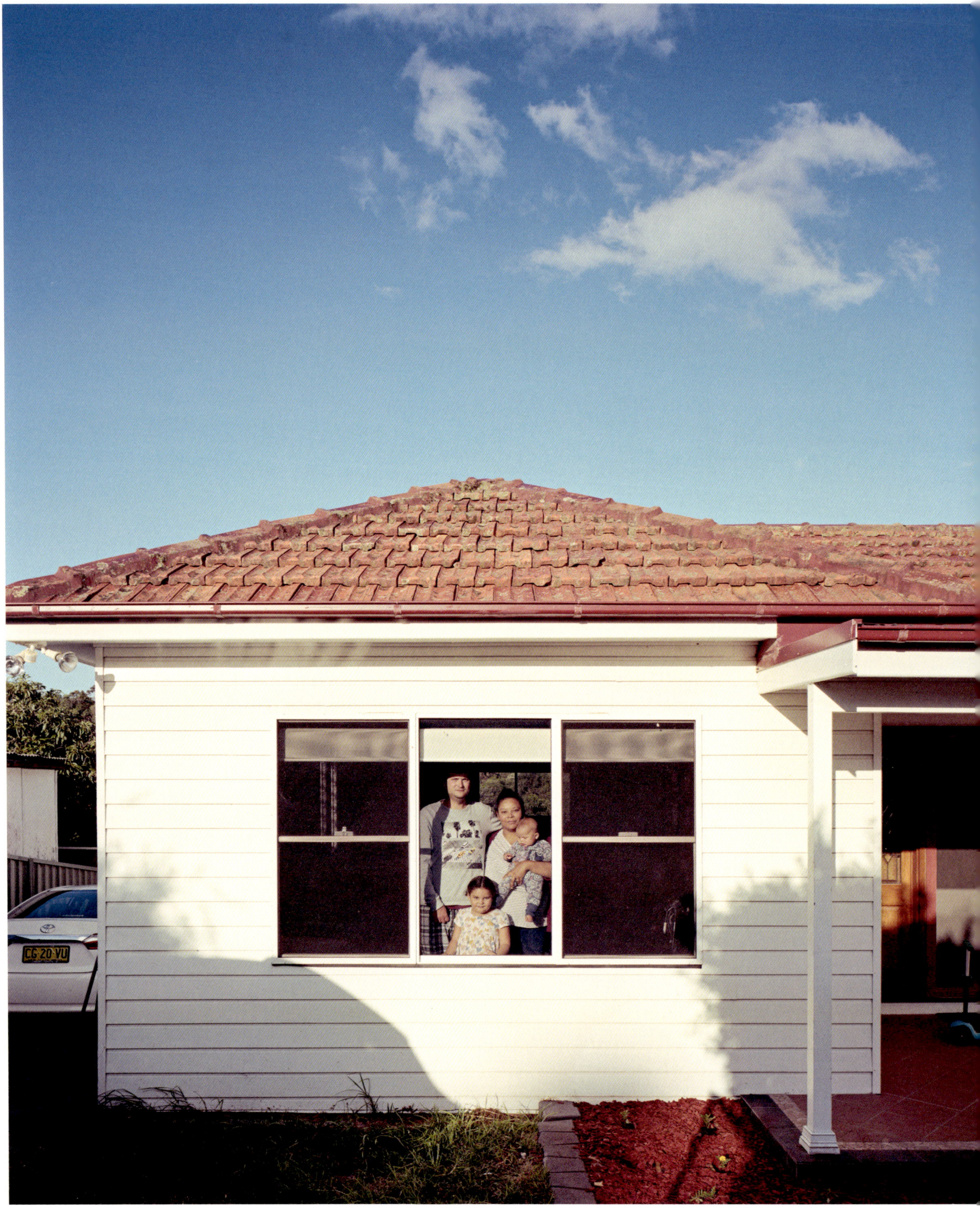
CG 20 VU

Katherine, Jonathon, Cecilia and Maria
3:23pm, 1 May 2020

Andy, Emily, and River
4:32pm, 21 April 2020

FOLLOWING LEFT
Alex and Wednesday
3:40pm, 29 April 2020

FOLLOWING RIGHT
Ray, Kimberly, Aliah, Alyssa and Amiia
3:32pm, 28 April 2020

GATEFOLD FROM LEFT TO RIGHT
Carol, Peter and Alexander
4:22pm, 30 August 2021

Stephen, Wendy and Gisela
4:29pm, 23 August 2021

Trevor and Jo
3:36pm, 10 August 2021

Theresa, David, DJ, Lauchlan, Max, Tiara,
Samuel, Preston, Logan and Sara
6:05pm, 6 October 2021

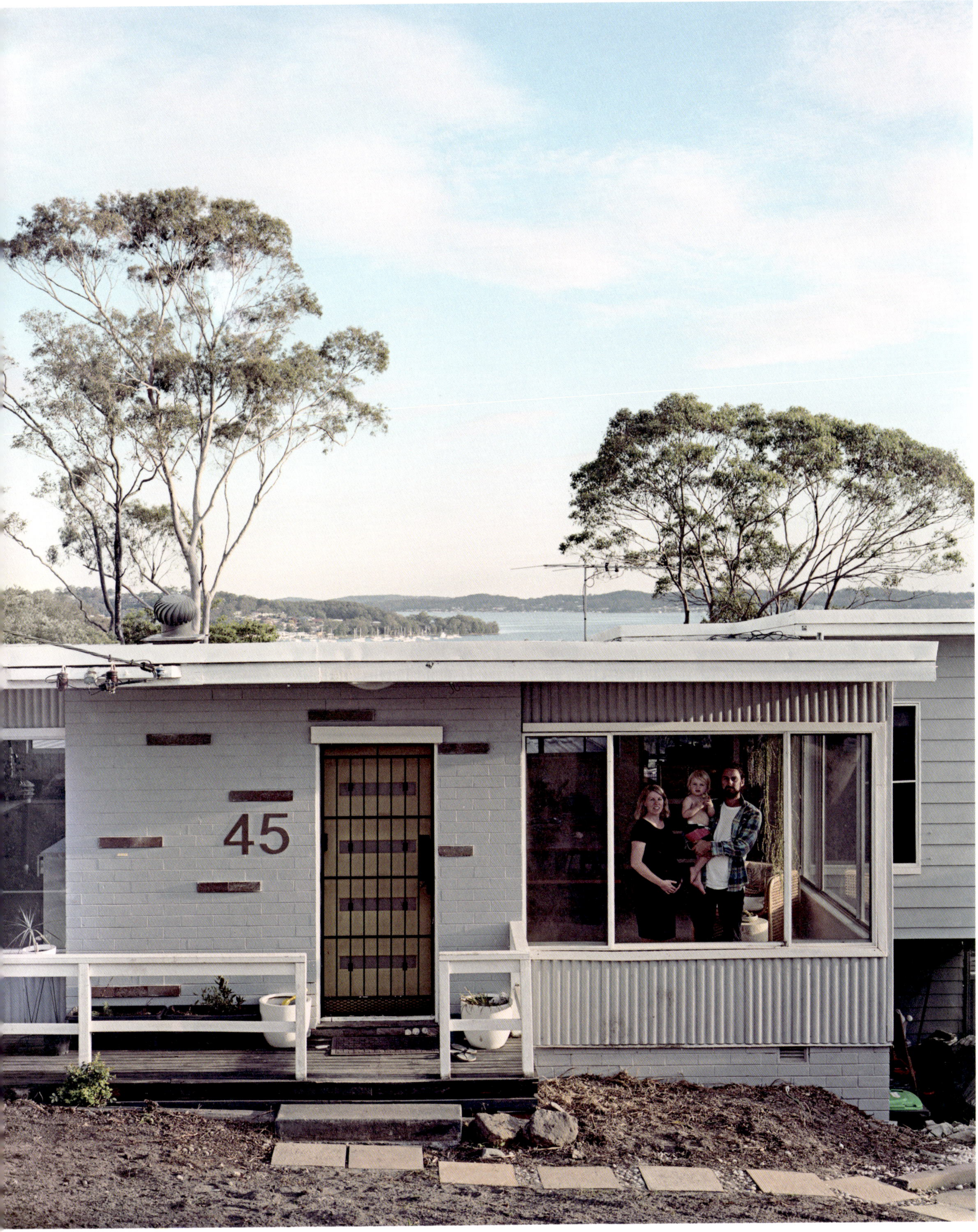
45

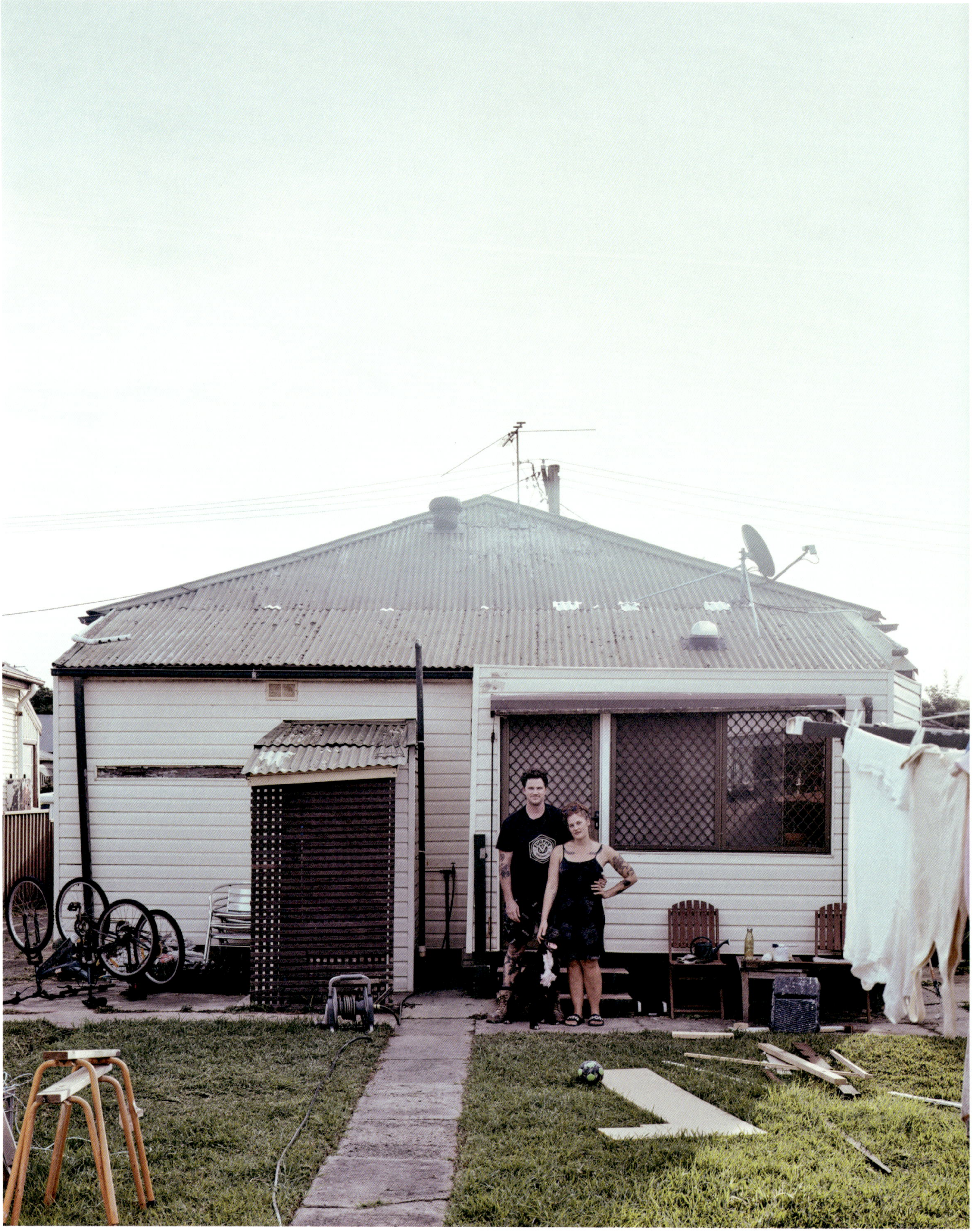

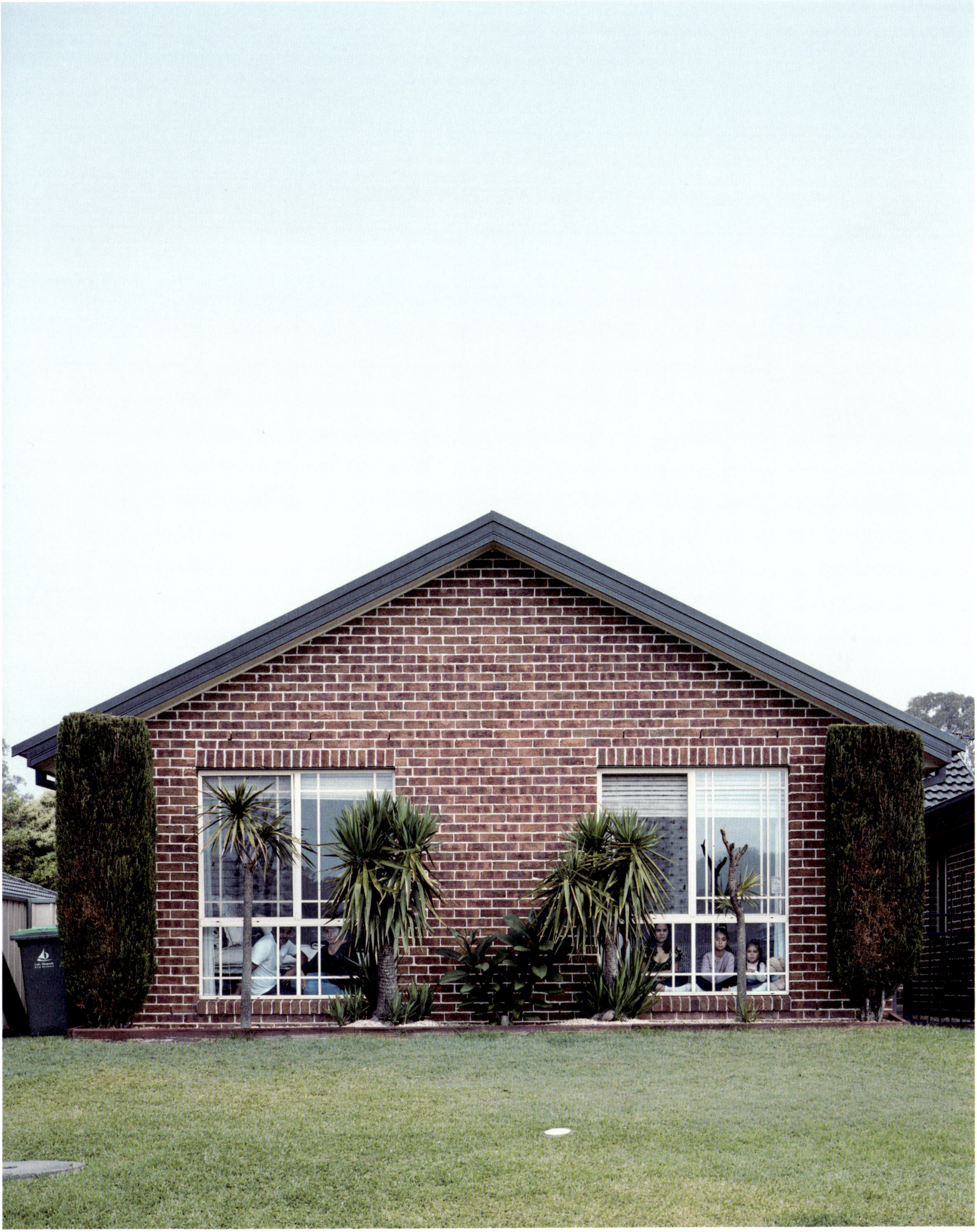

Forugh and his wife, daughters and son
5:00pm, 24 September 2021

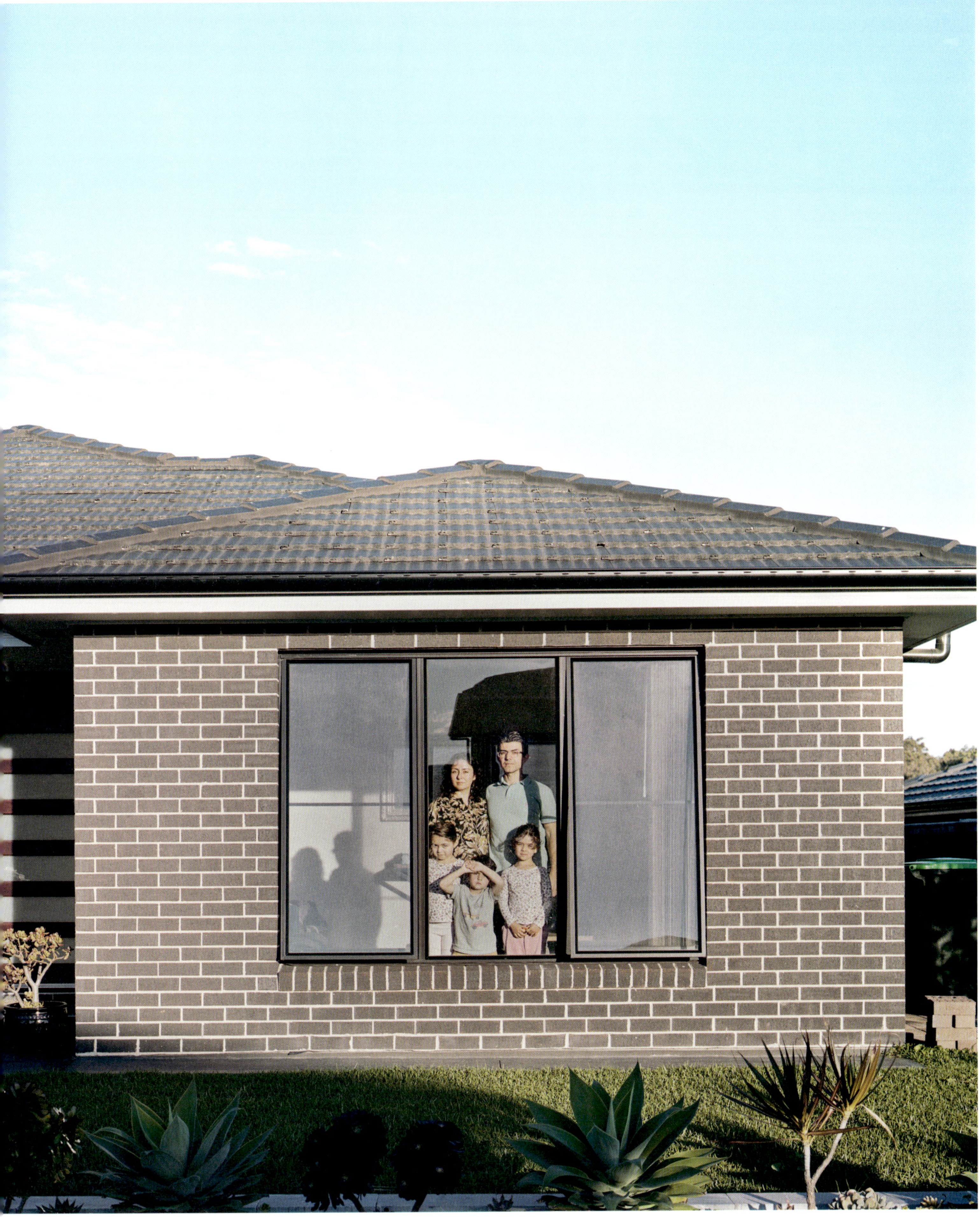

Mohamed
4:25pm, 13 August 2021

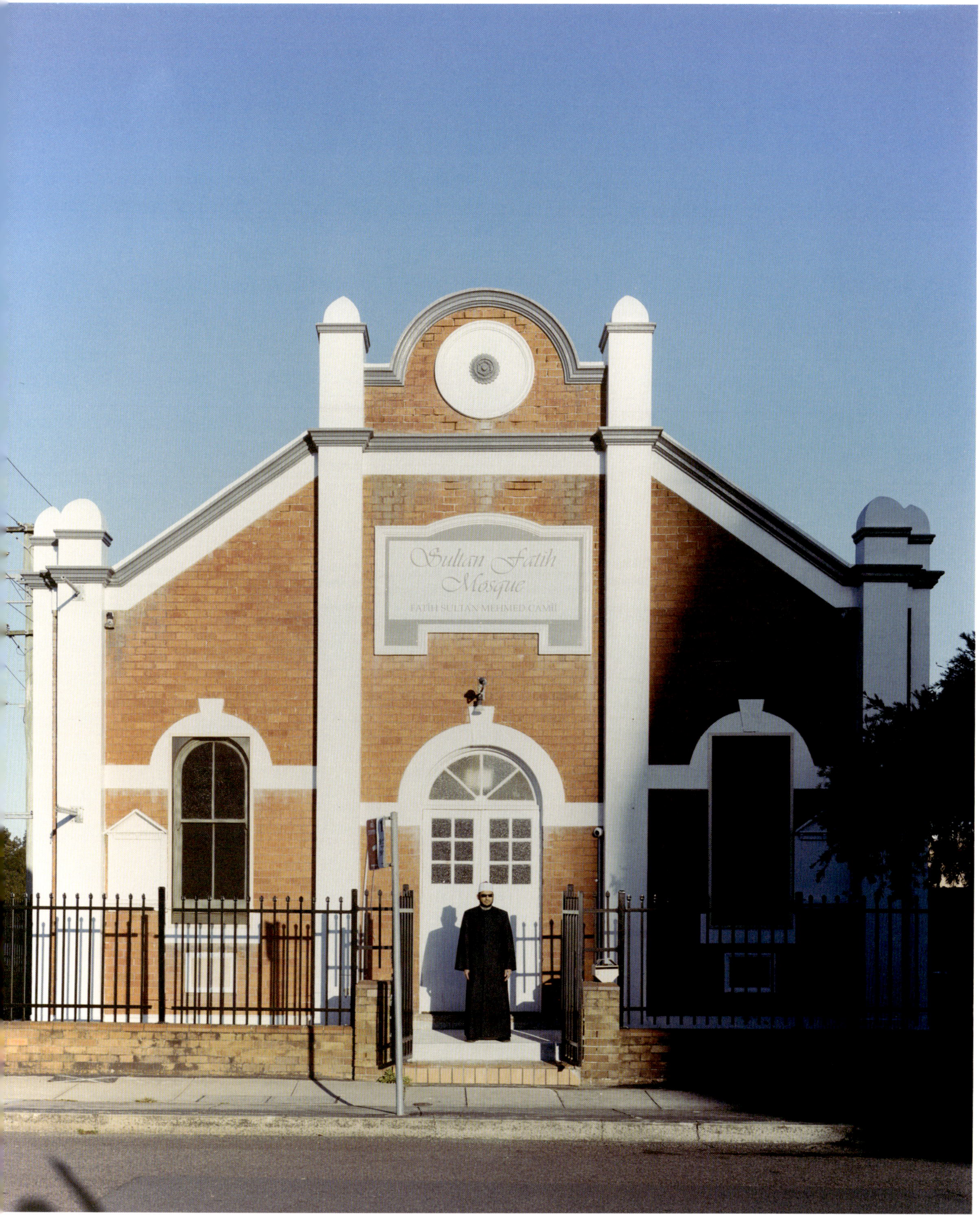
Sultan Fatih
Mosque
FATIH SULTAN MEHMED CAMII

Sophie, Aaron, Reuben and Sidney
3:44pm, 25 April 2020

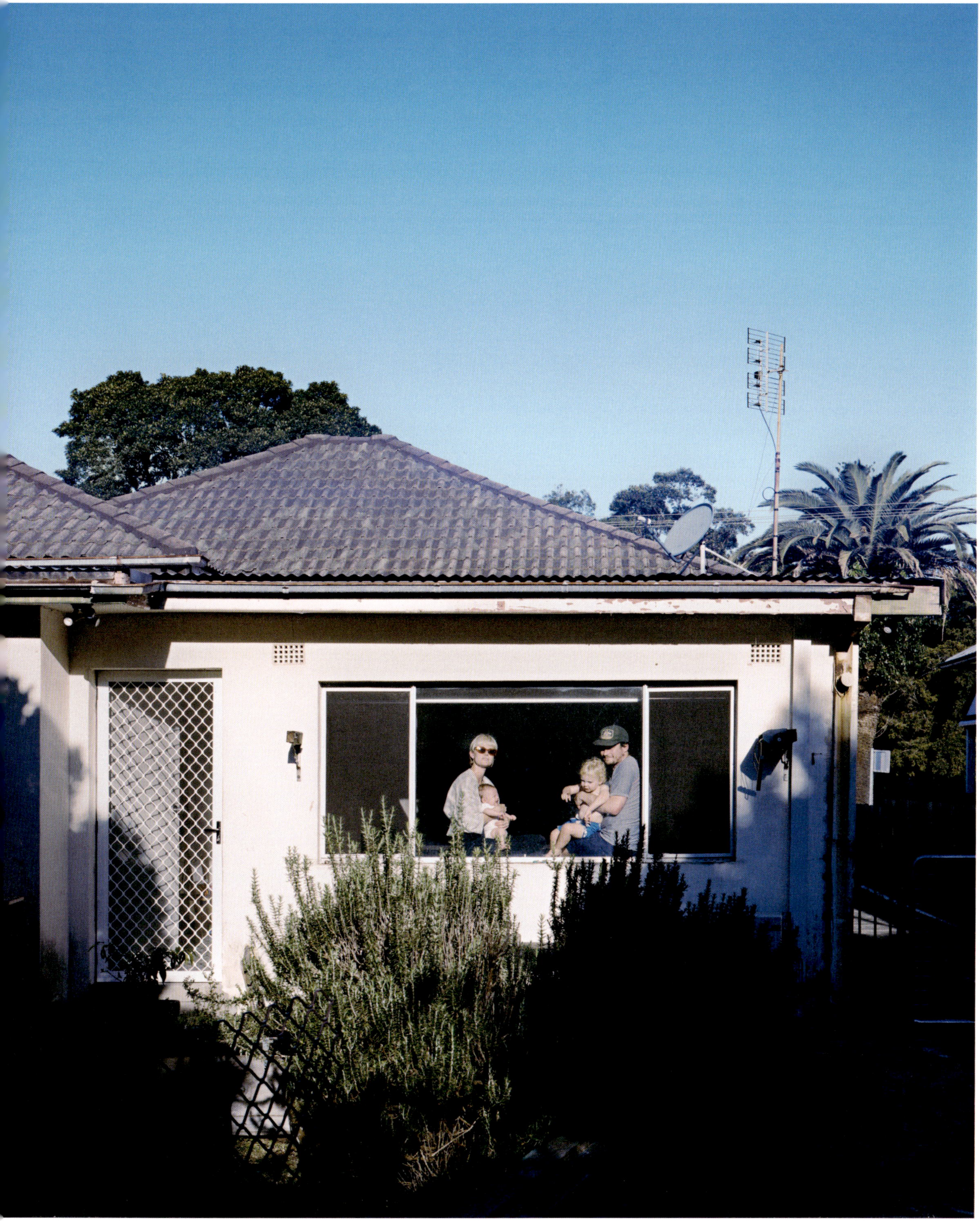

Jess, Wayne, Tyrone,
Kayden and Makaylah
3:40pm, 31 August 2021

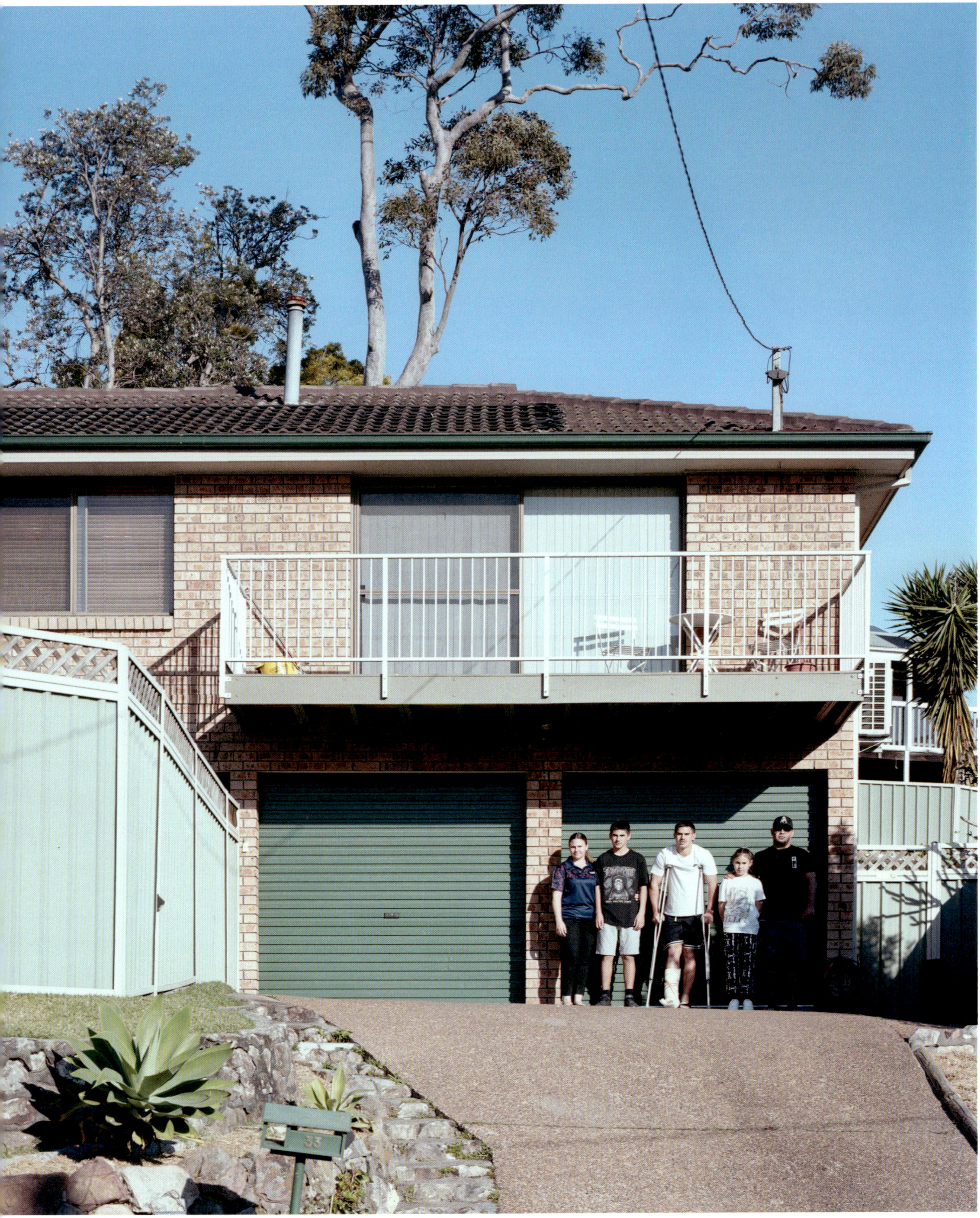
33

Mario, Liz, Victoria and Curtis
2:25pm, 24 April 2020

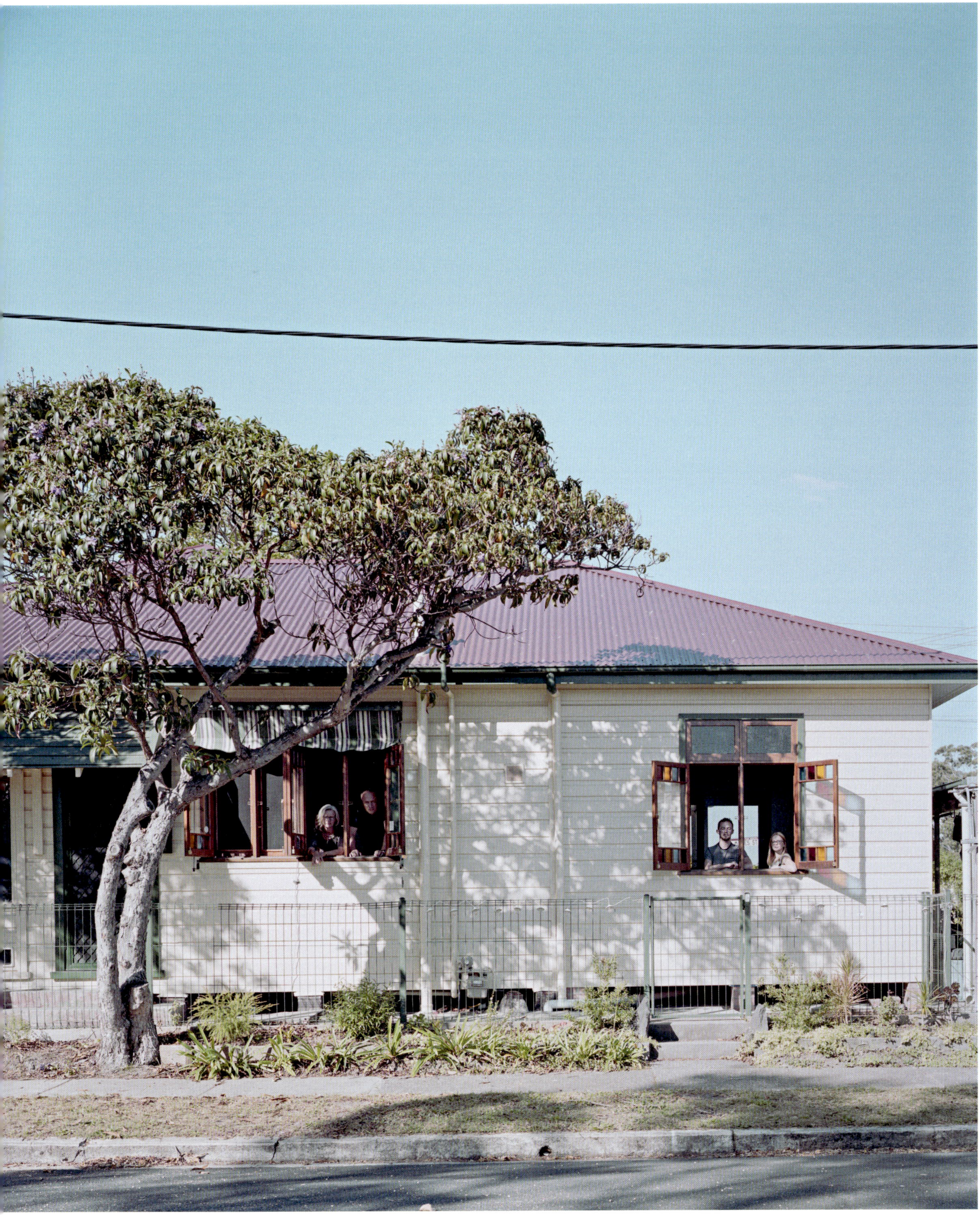

Thomas, Laura and Eden
4:48pm, 6 October 2021

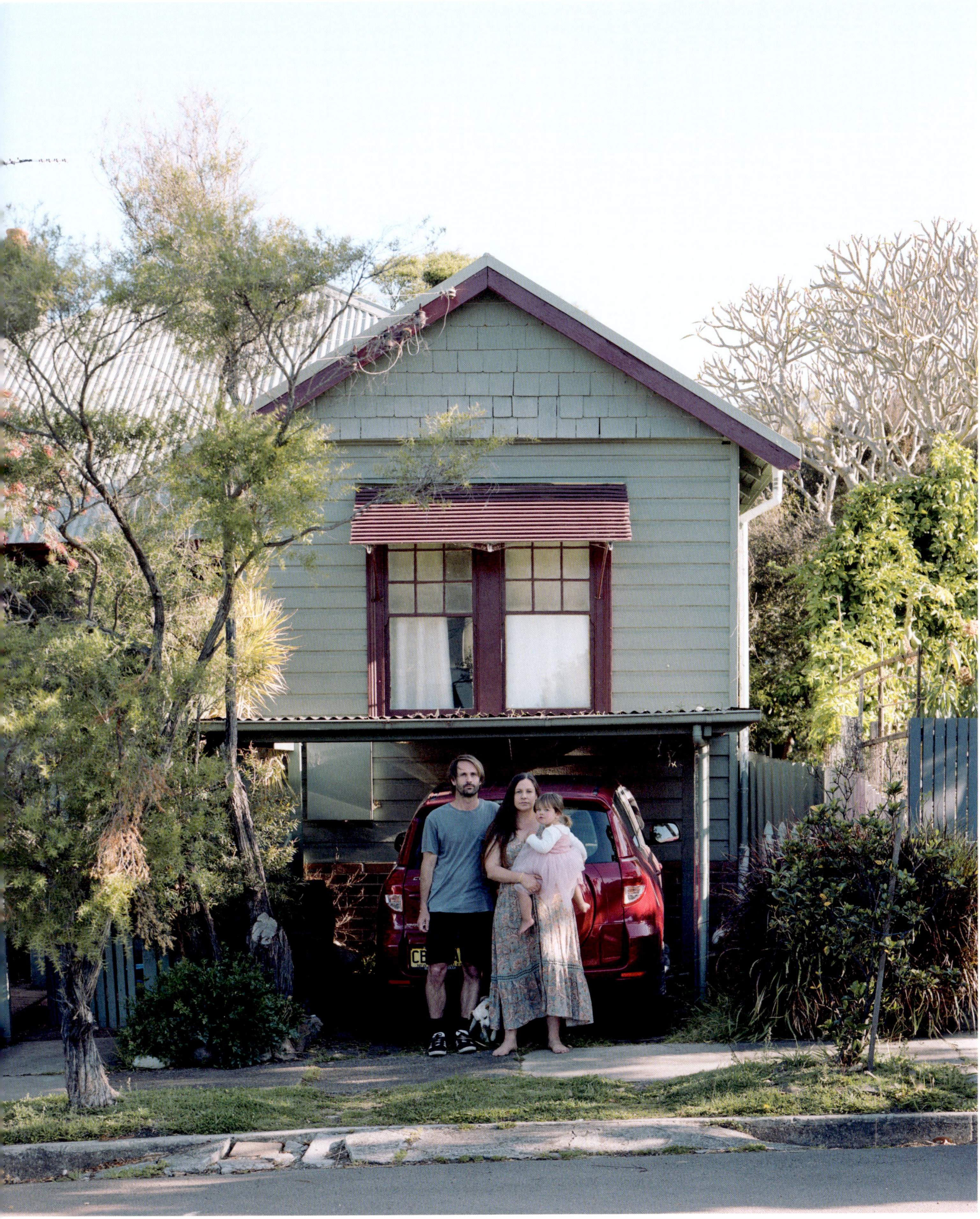

Jordan, Keelan, Charlee,
Rhian and Liam
3:36pm, 27 April 2020

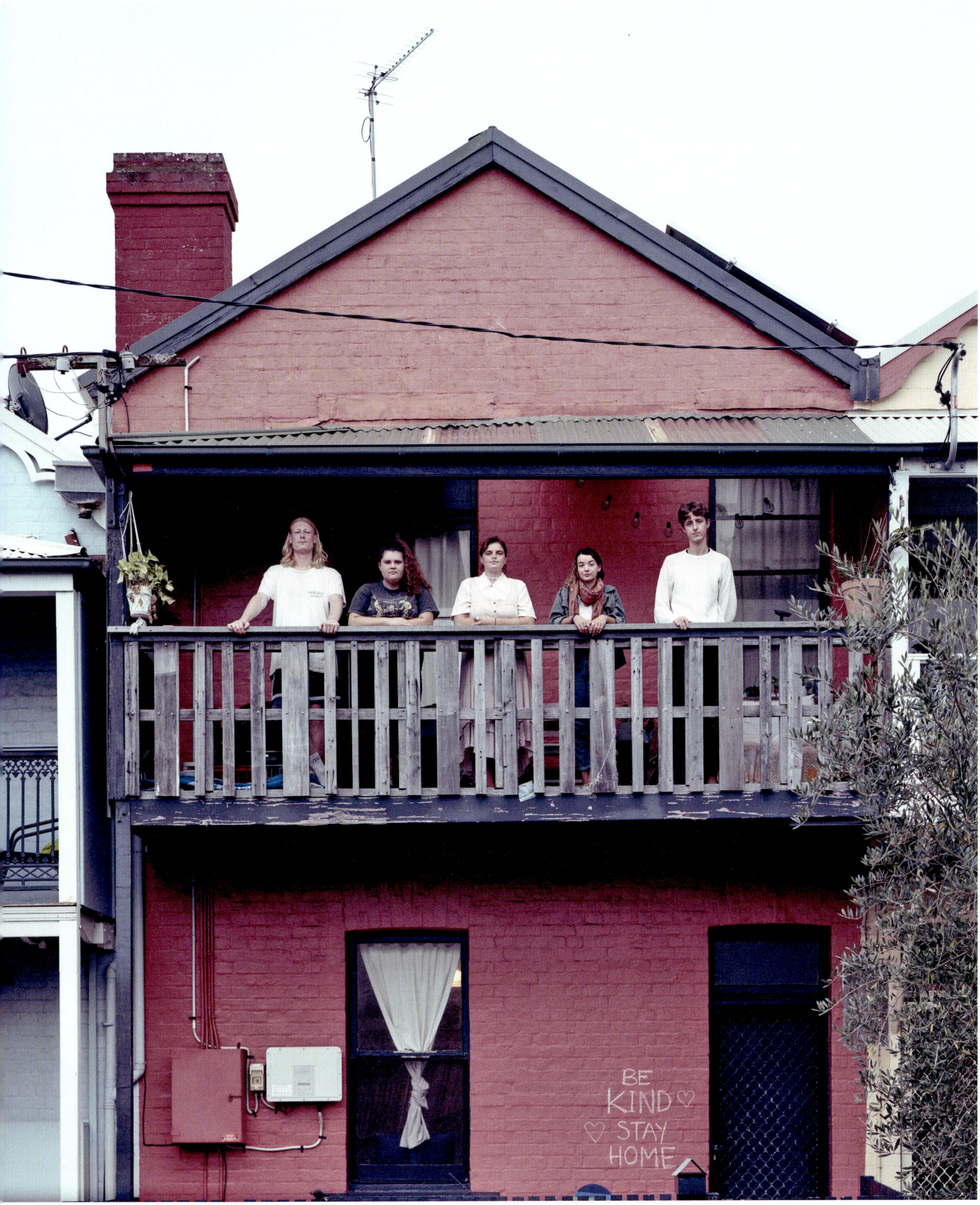
BE
KIND
STAY
HOME

Zana and Patrick
4:27pm, 31 May 2020

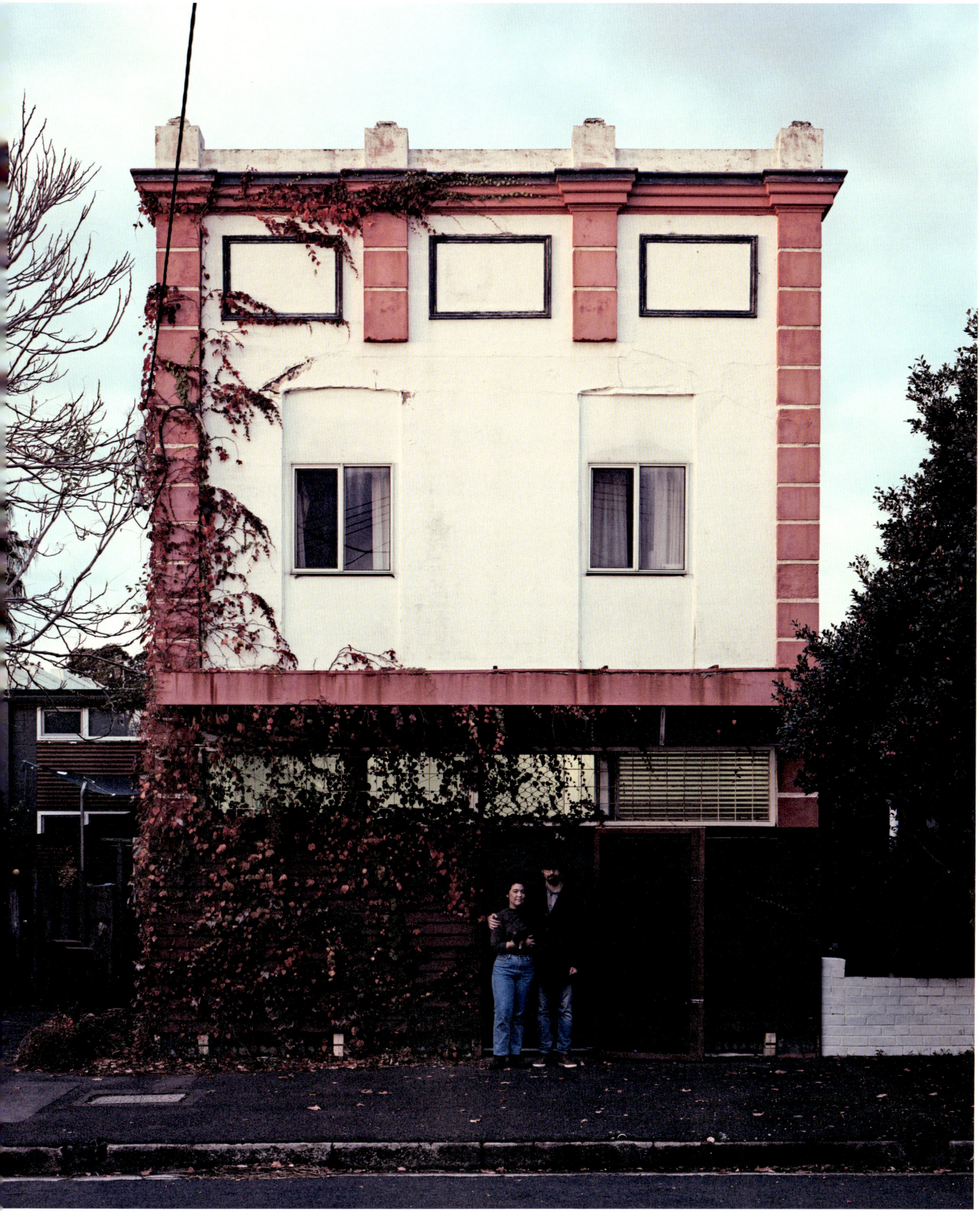

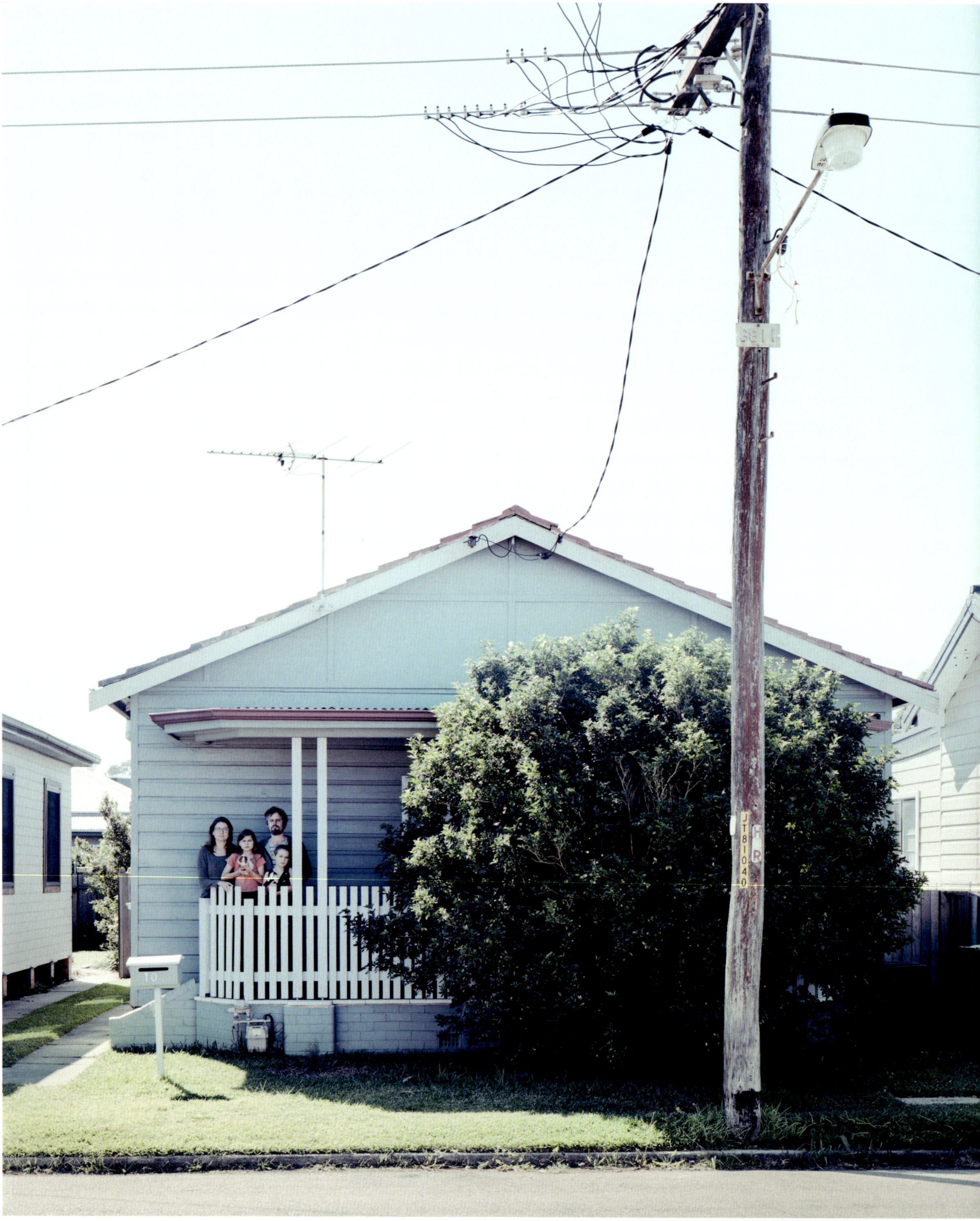

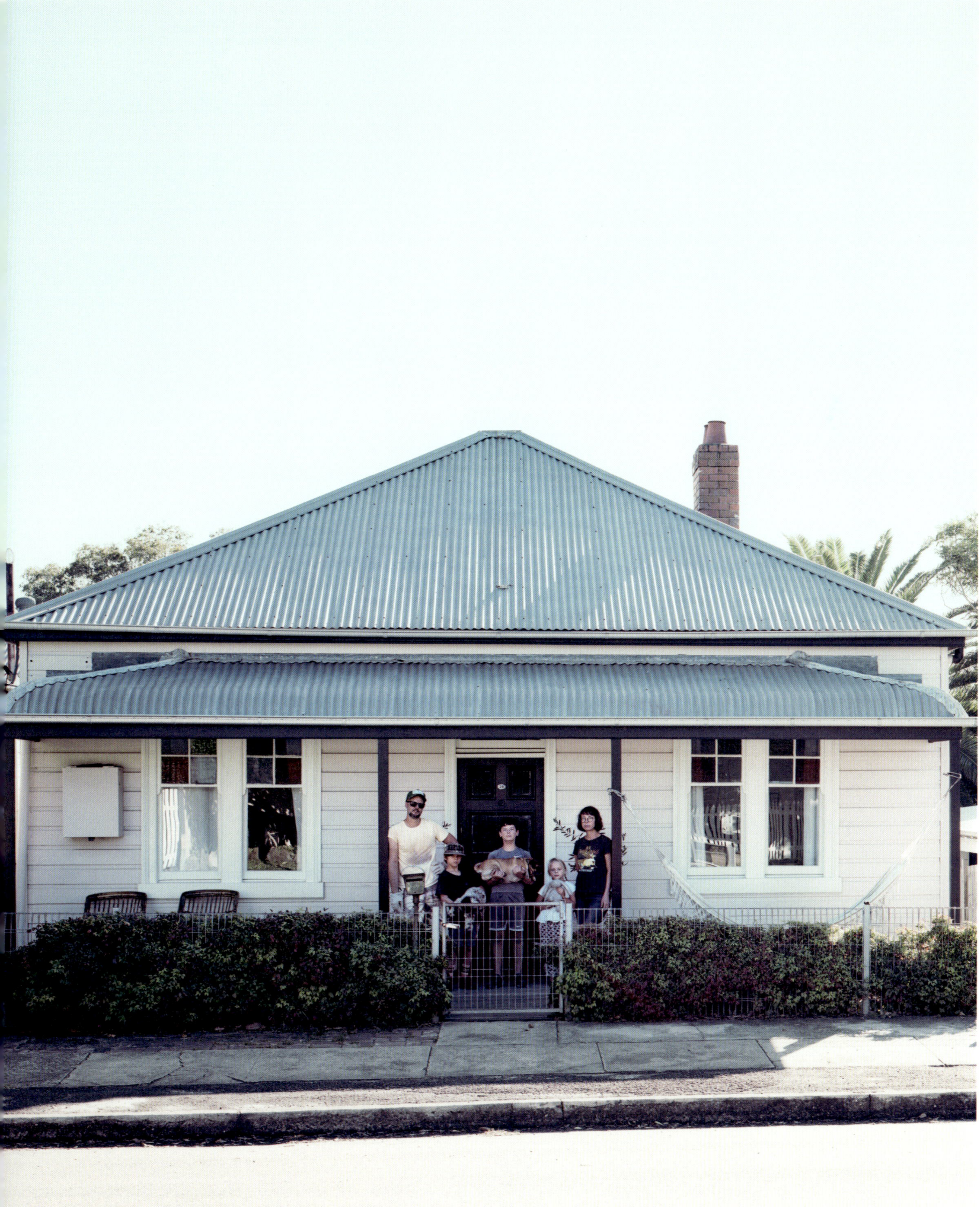

PREVIOUS LEFT
Chelsey, Chris, Izzy and Lara
1:34pm, 23 April 2020

PREVIOUS RIGHT
Courtney, Adam, Oli, Charlie
and Francesca
4:36pm, 30 May 2020

Kieran, Renae and Iris
4:36pm, 30 May 2020

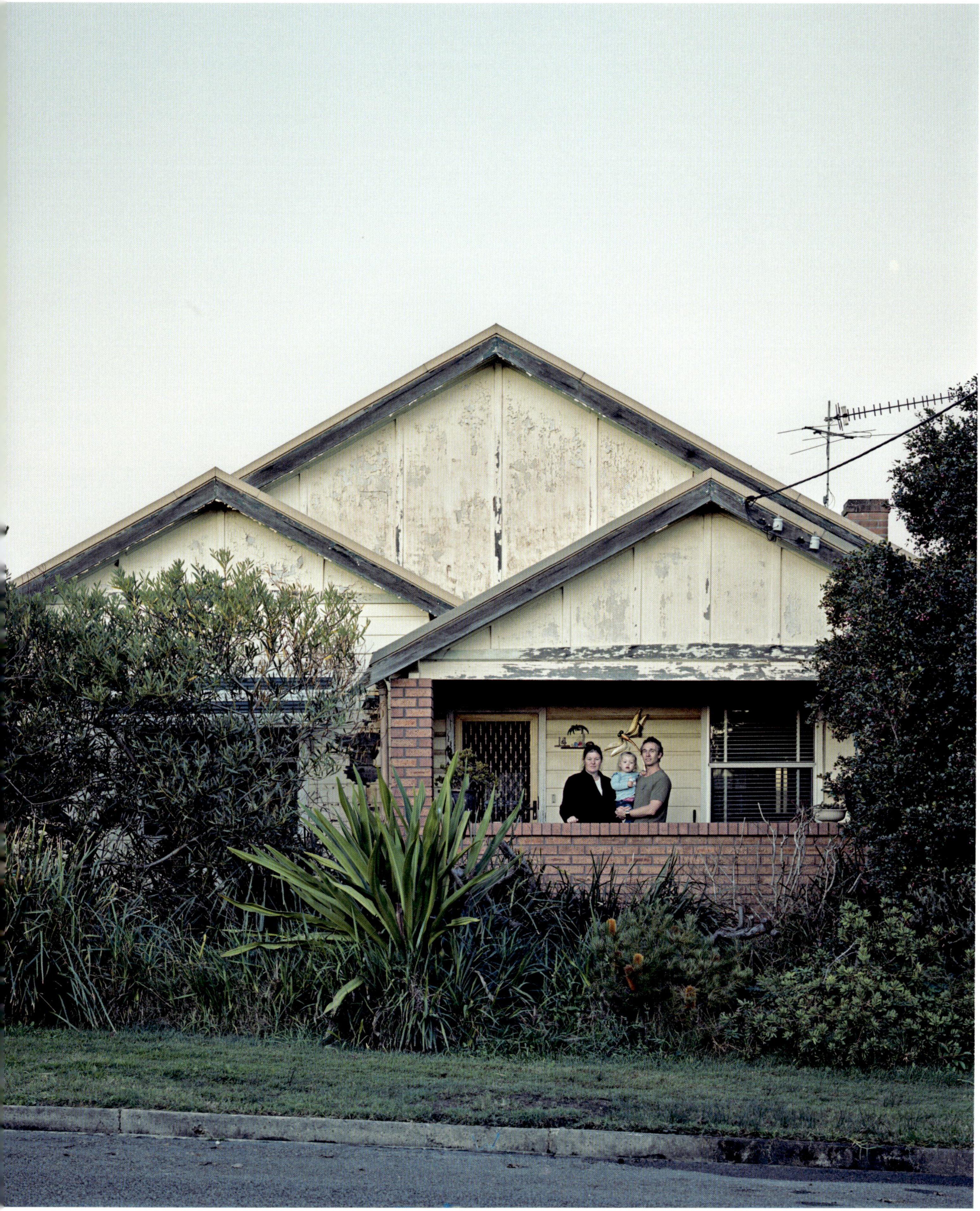

Jacqui, Ben, Max and Helen
3:31pm, 22 May 2020

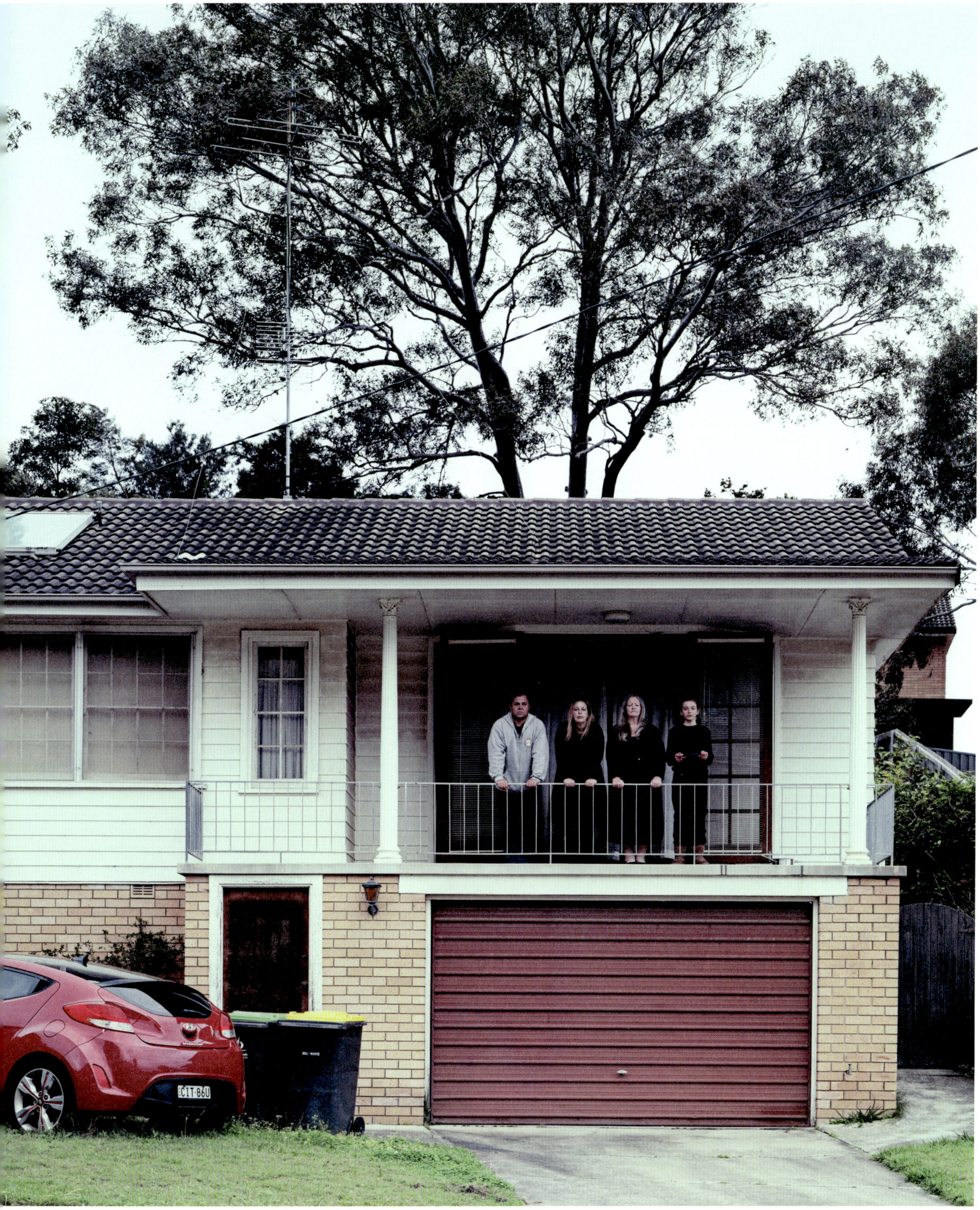

David, Tamara, Lily and Flynn
5:01pm, 23 September 2021

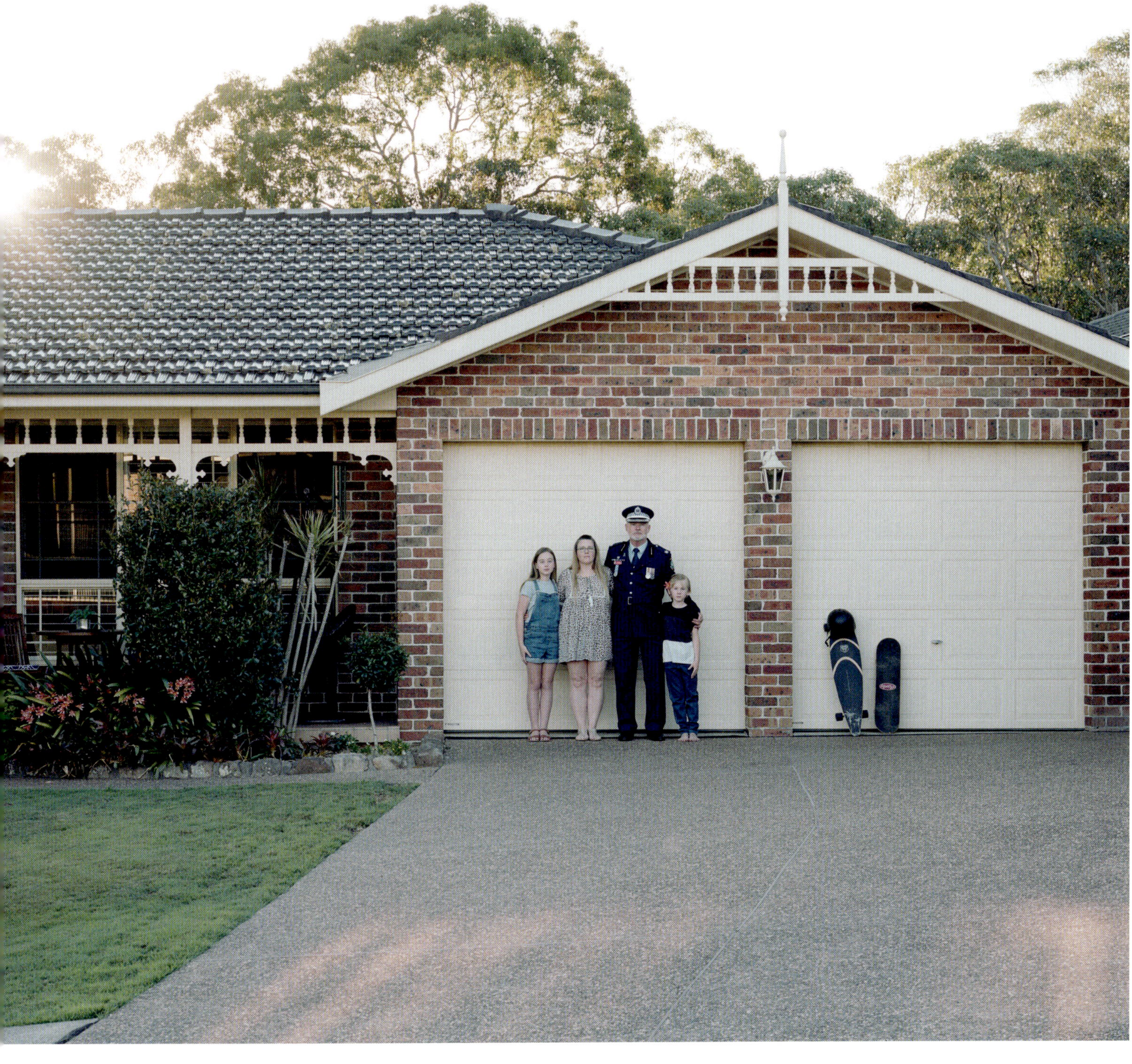

Max and Heather
4:32pm, 7 September 2021

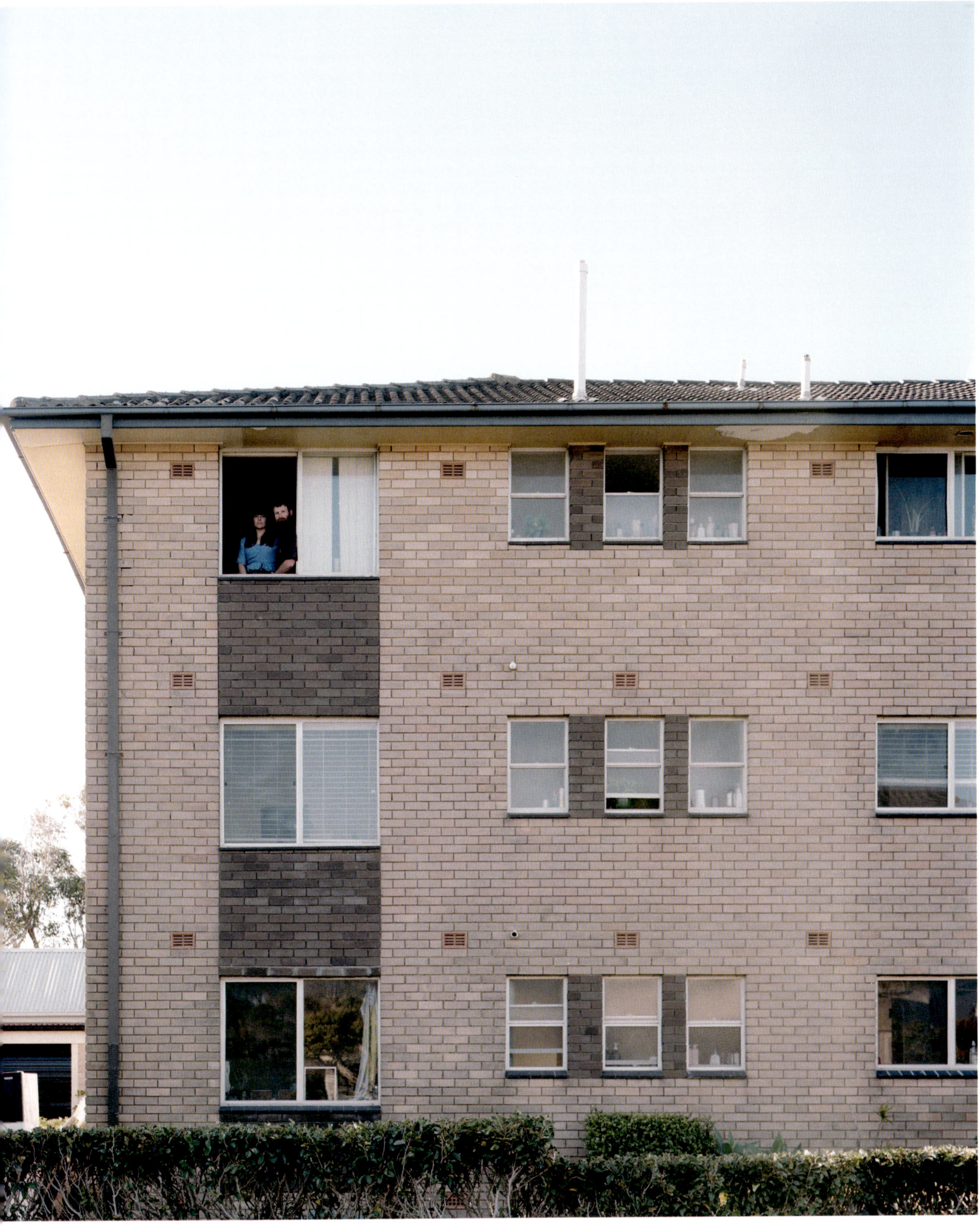

Greg
1:15pm, 7 May 2020

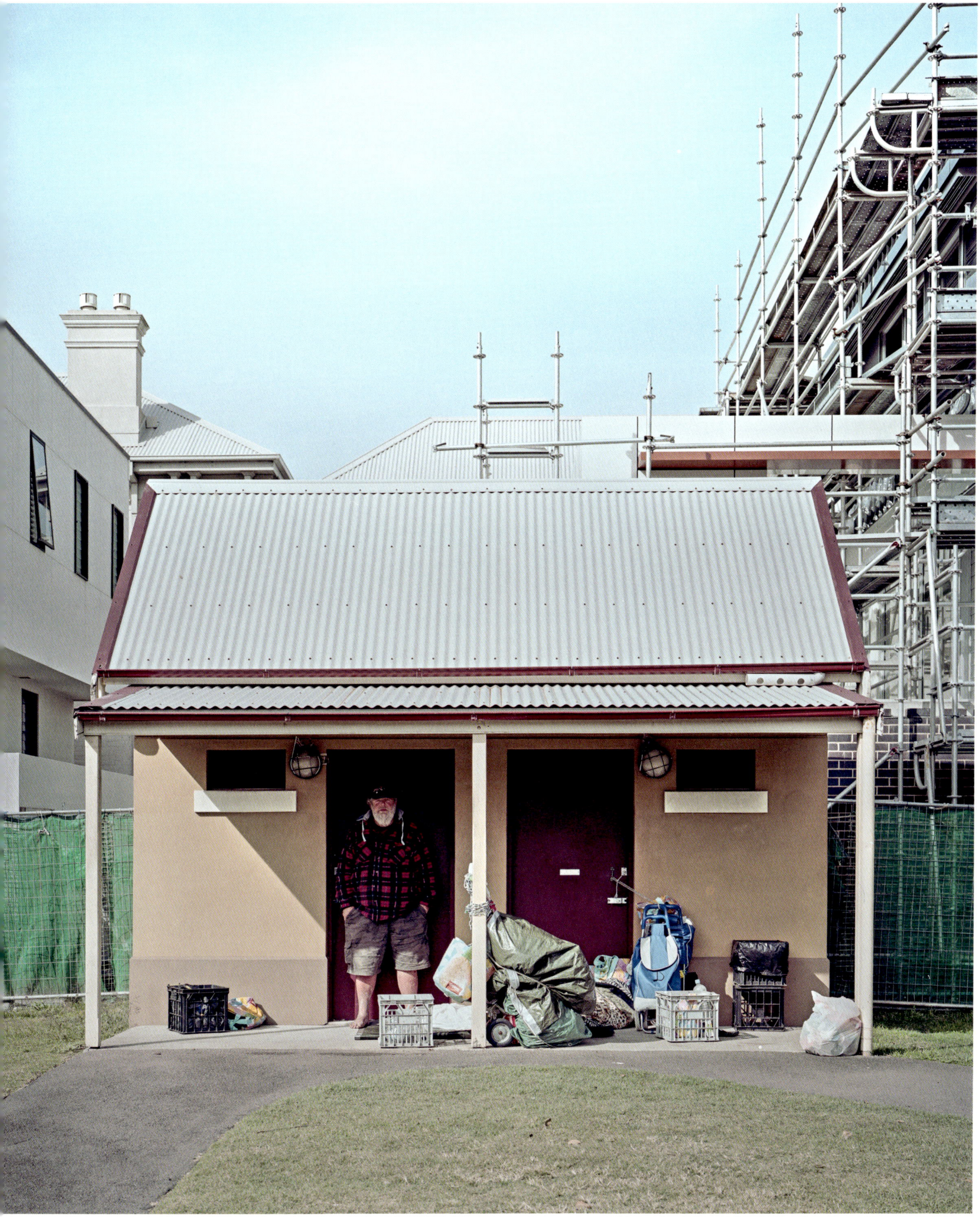

Nuatali, Stuart, Archie, Stella-Rose
and Ruby-Lou
3:41pm, 28 August 2021

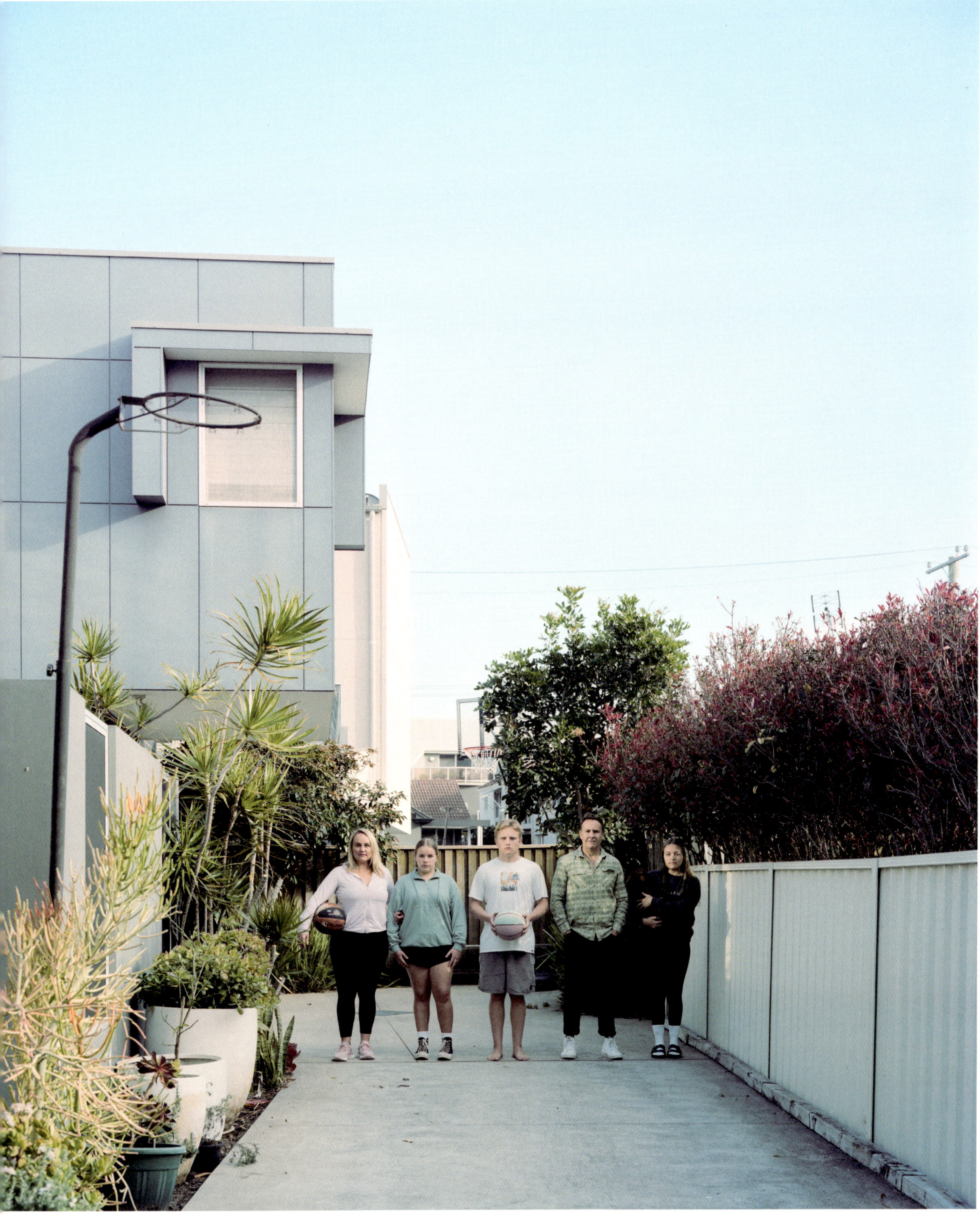

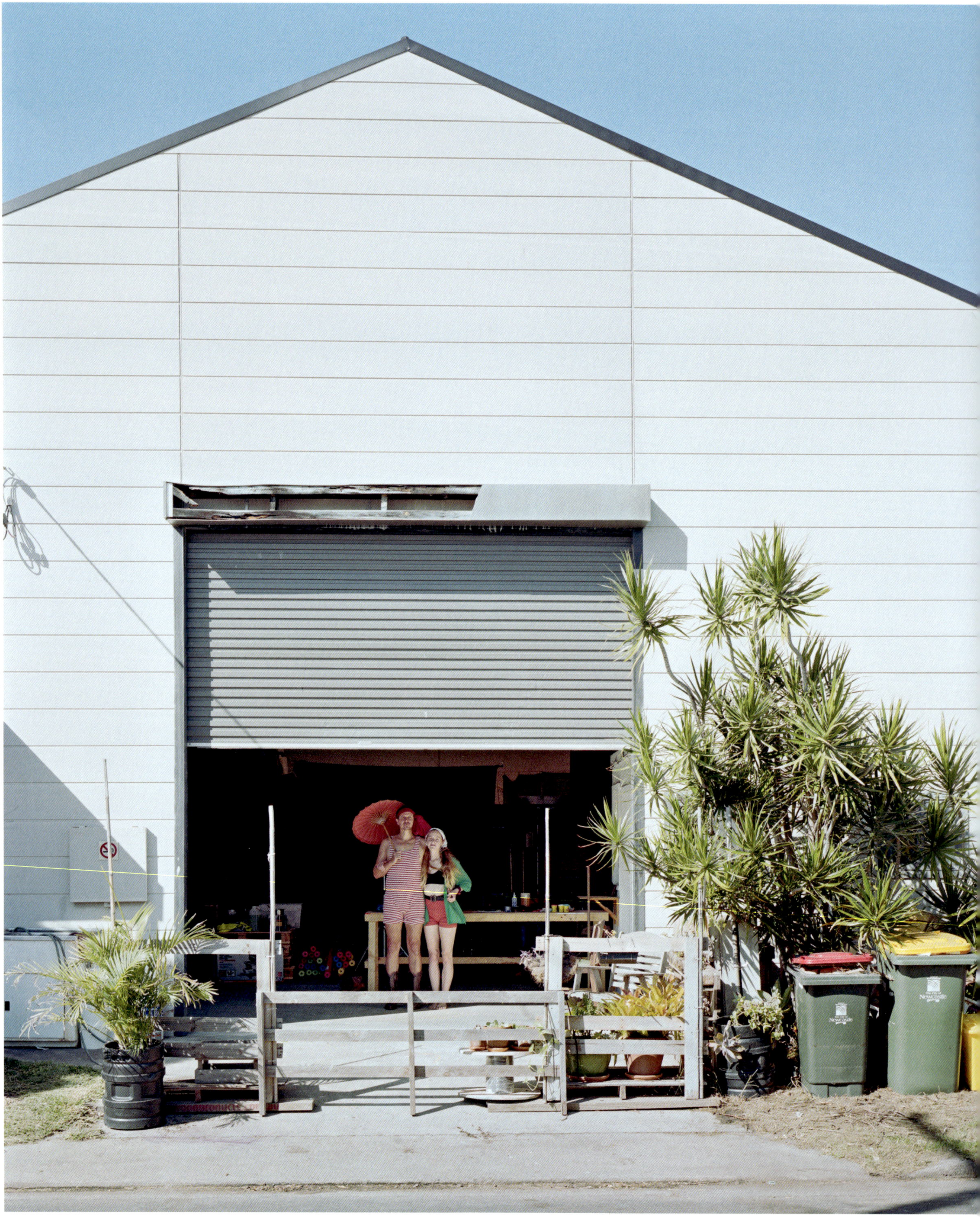

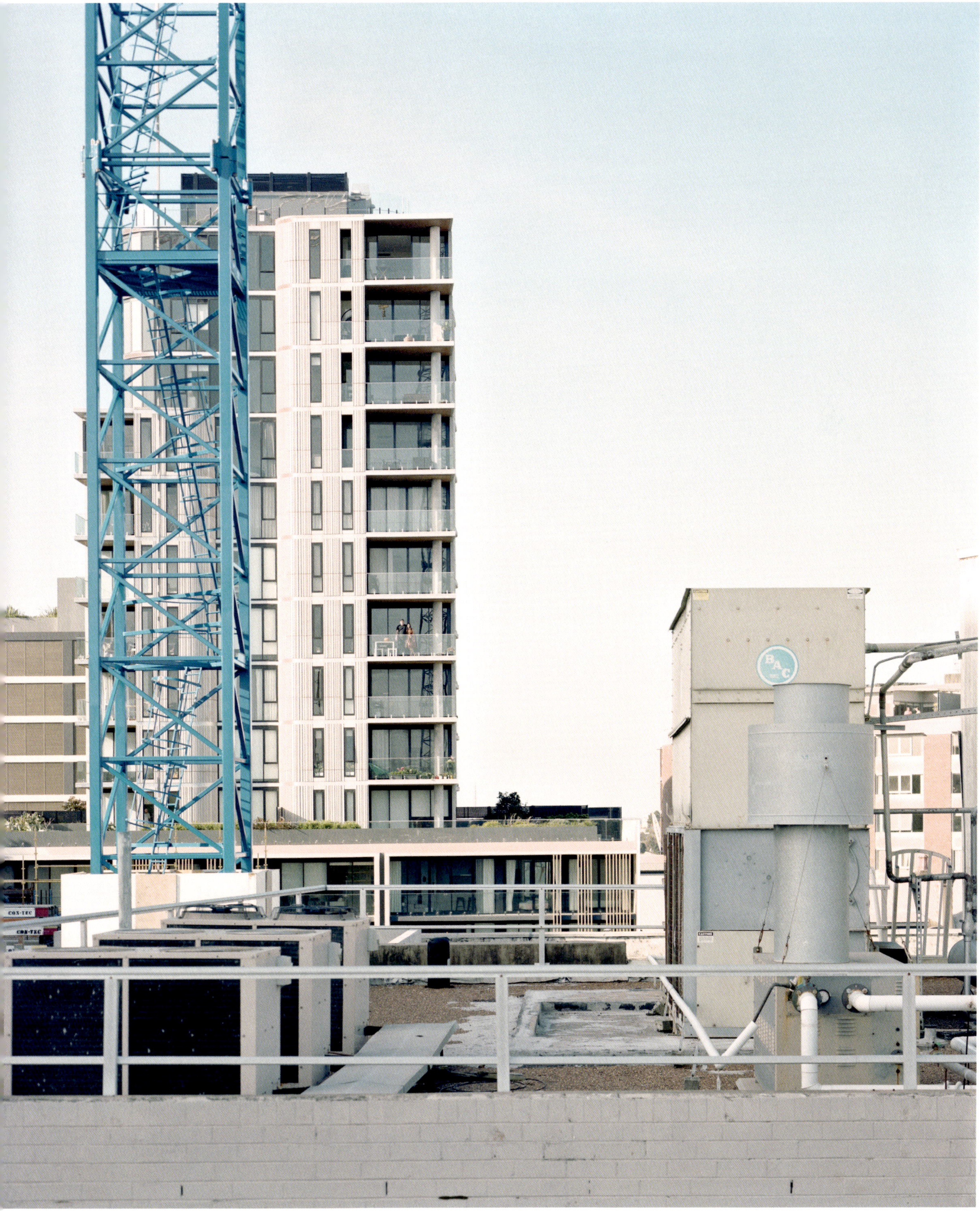
BAC

PREVIOUS LEFT
Marigold and Zack
1:15pm, 24 April 2020

PREVIOUS RIGHT
Alex and Josh
4:56pm, 8 October 2021

Simon
3:59pm, 22 August 2021

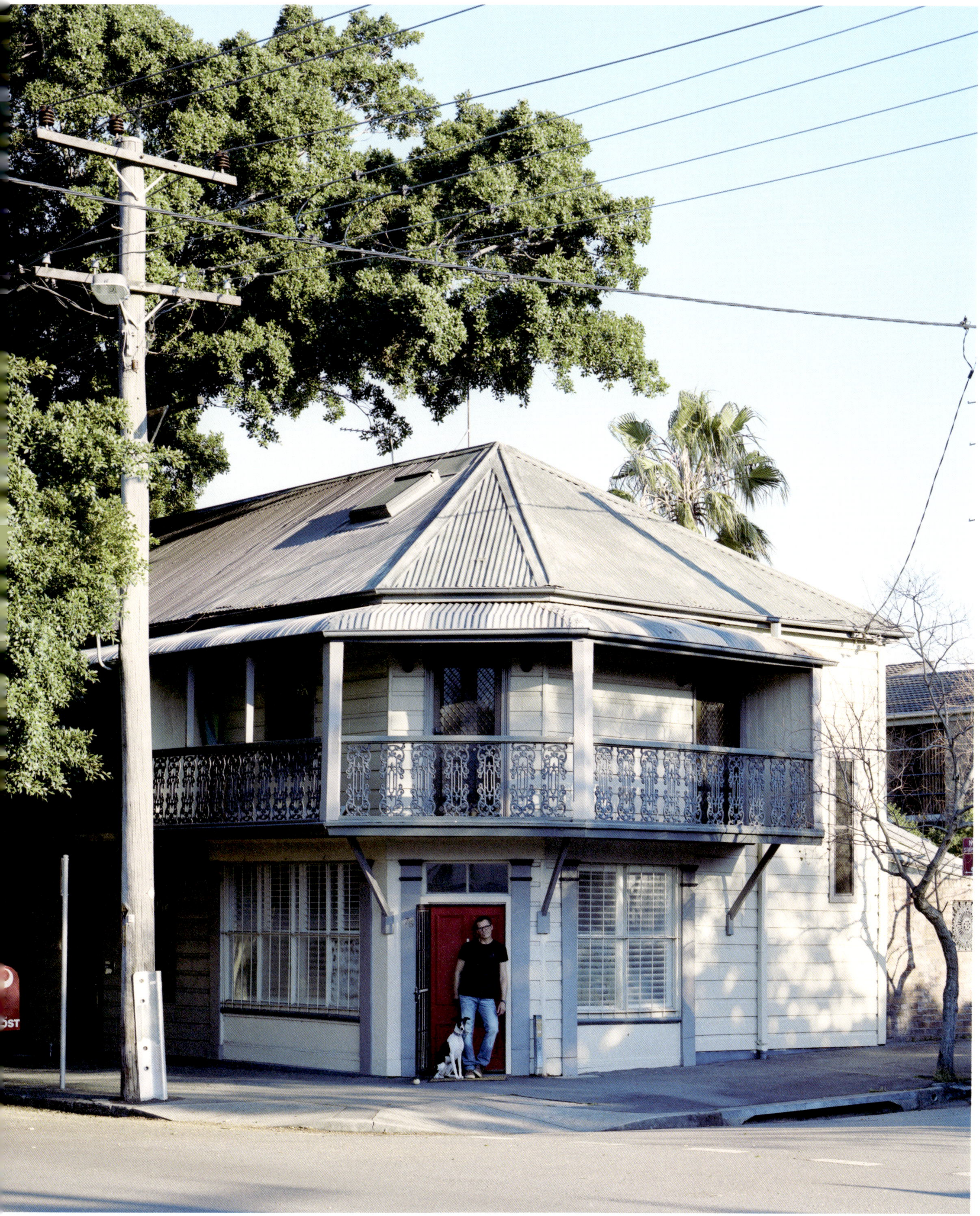

Mia, Phoebe, Ramona, Liam,
Tegan and Kirra
4:42pm, 21 August 2021

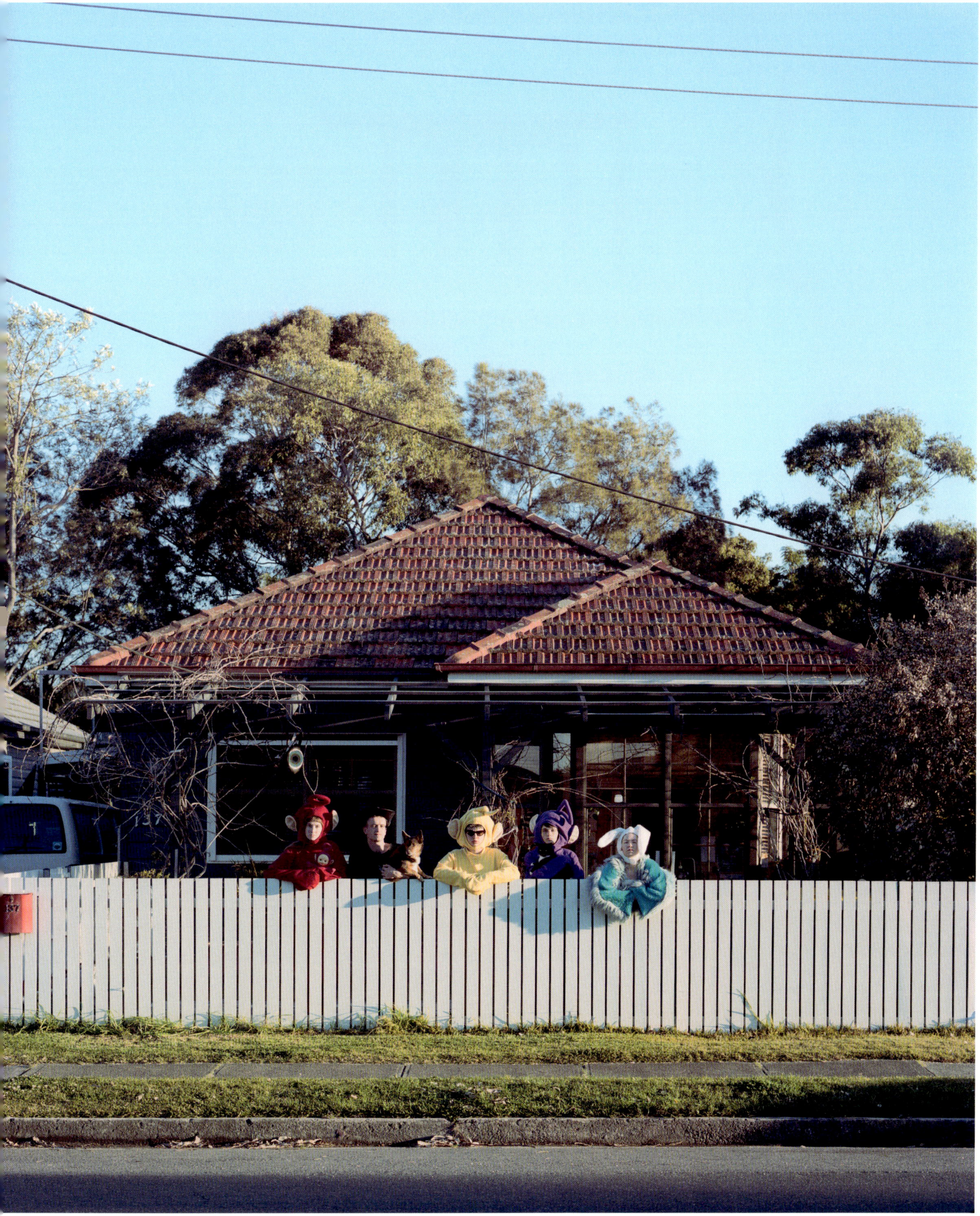

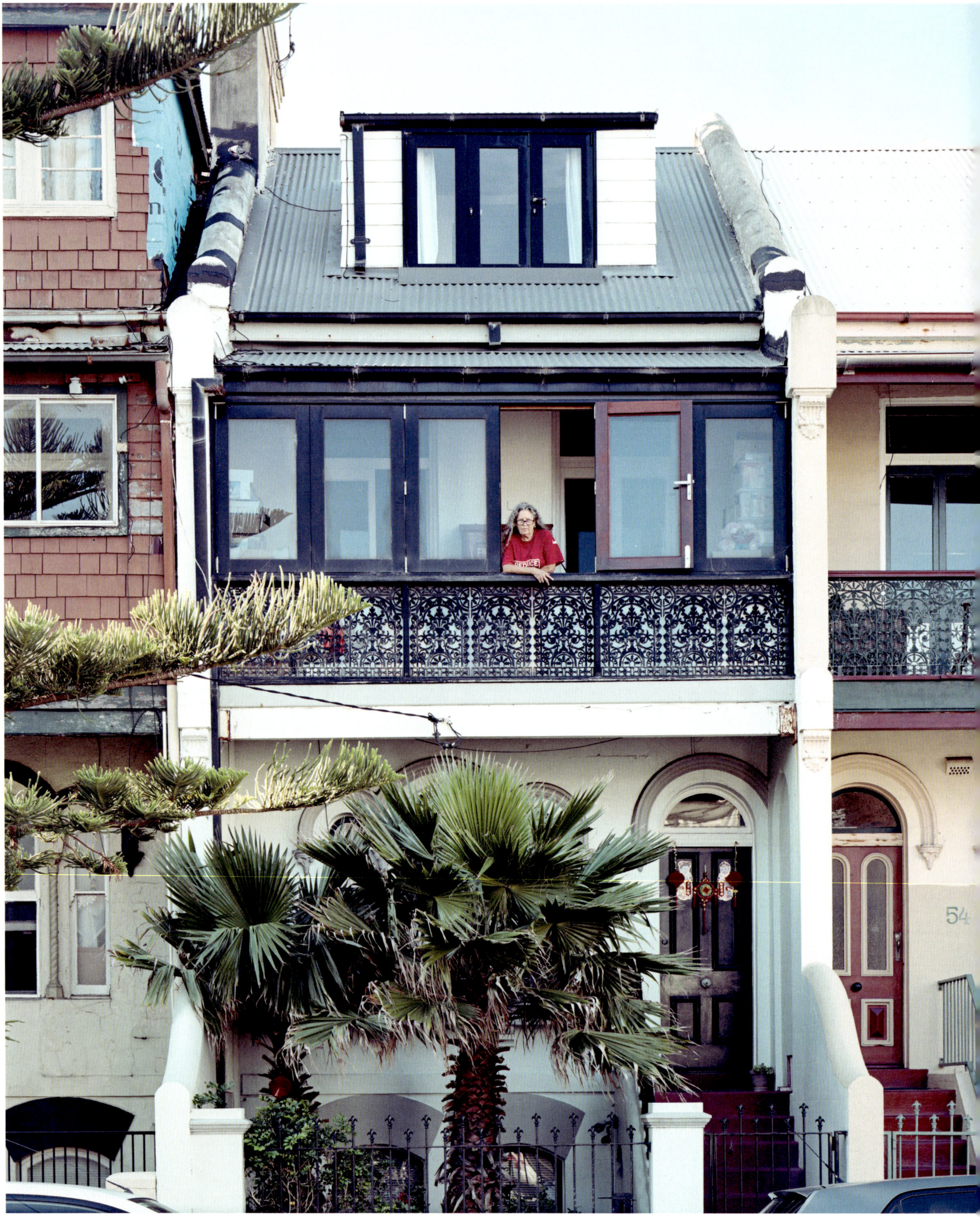
54

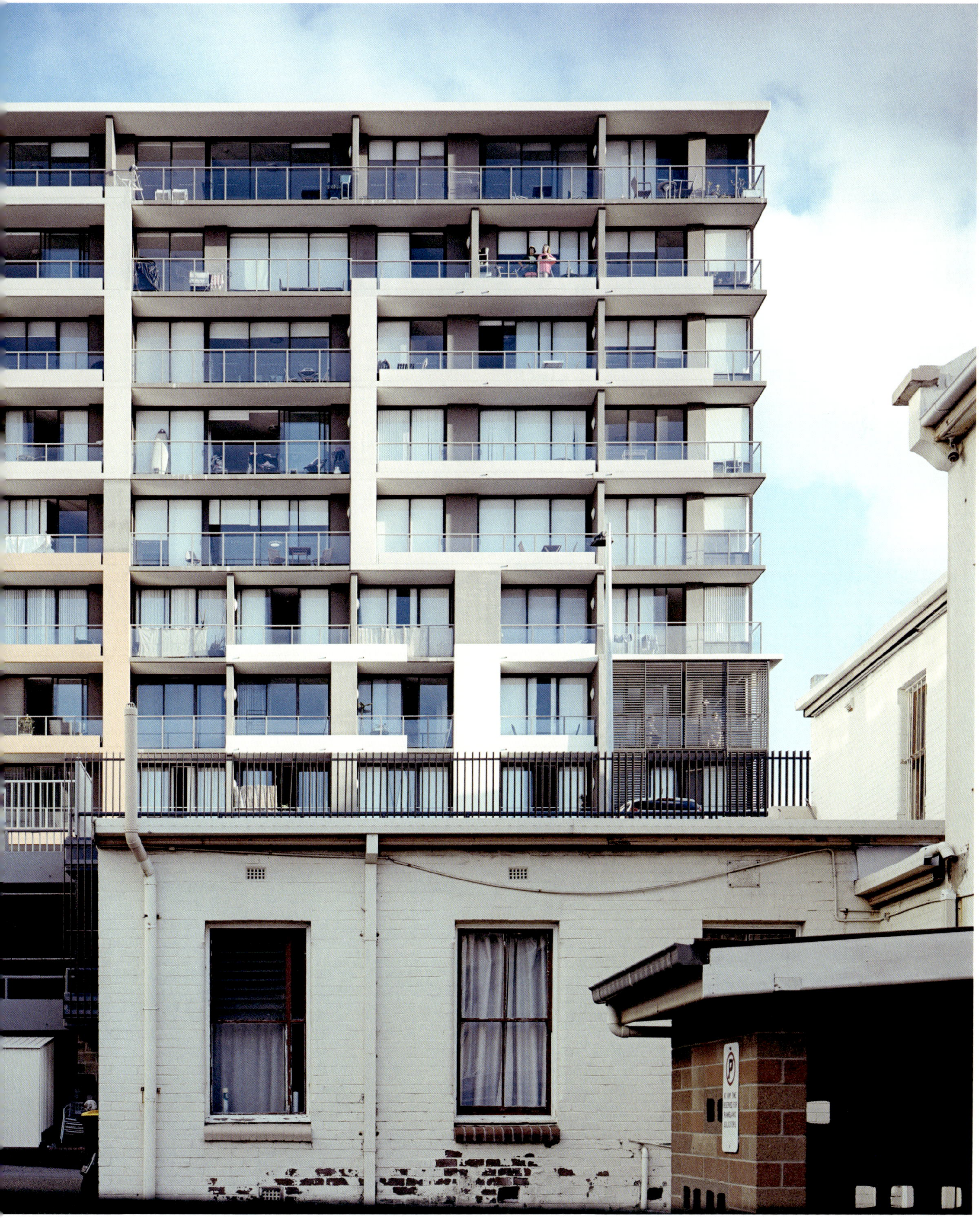

PREVIOUS LEFT
Catherine
1:15pm, 24 April 2020

PREVIOUS RIGHT
Helen and Bridget
4:14pm, 17 May 2020

Geordie, Eartha, Emmylou and Howlin
2:55pm, 17 April 2020

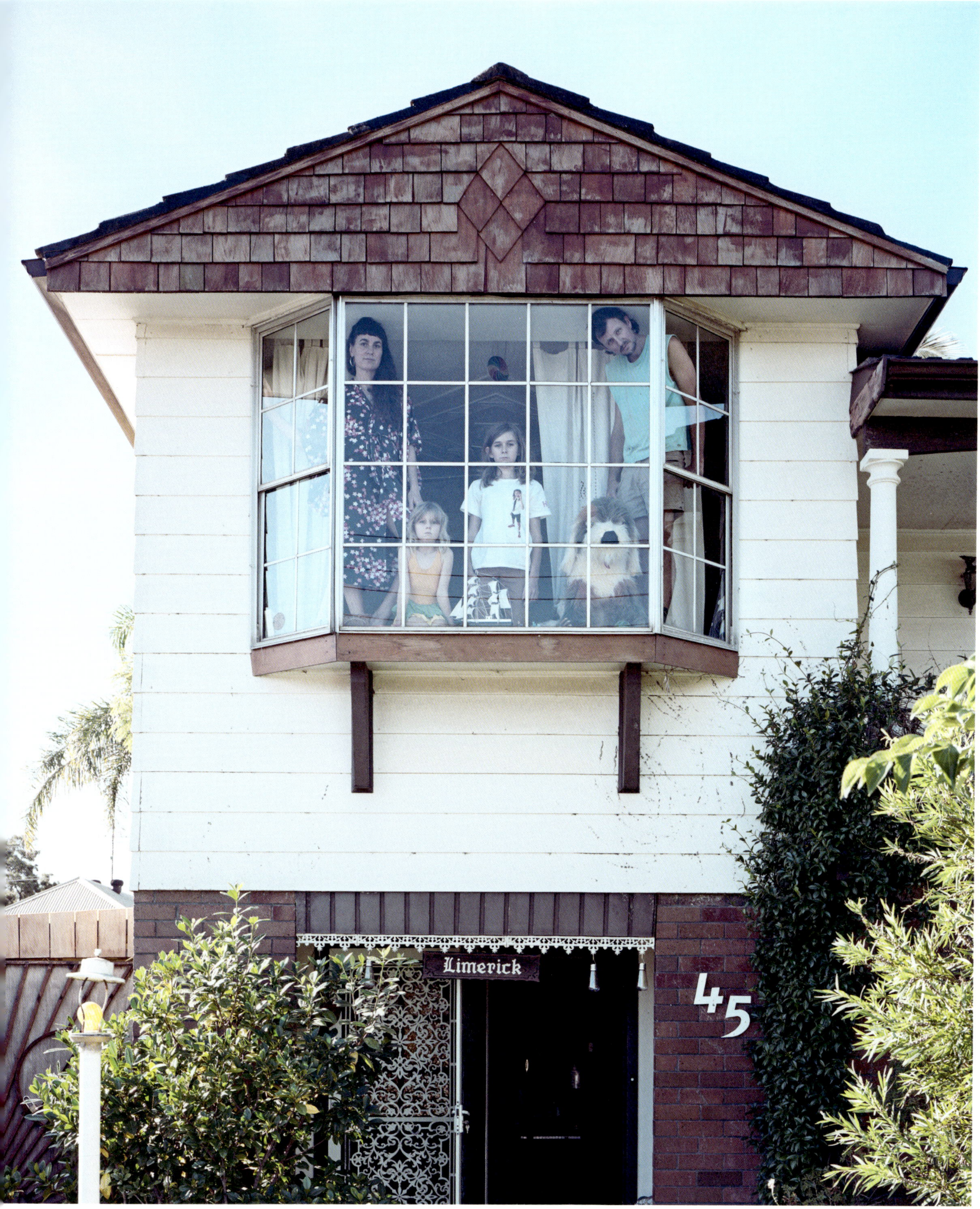
Limerick
45

Jeptha, Tegan, Kristen, Jerry
and Genevieve
4:40pm, 28 April 2020

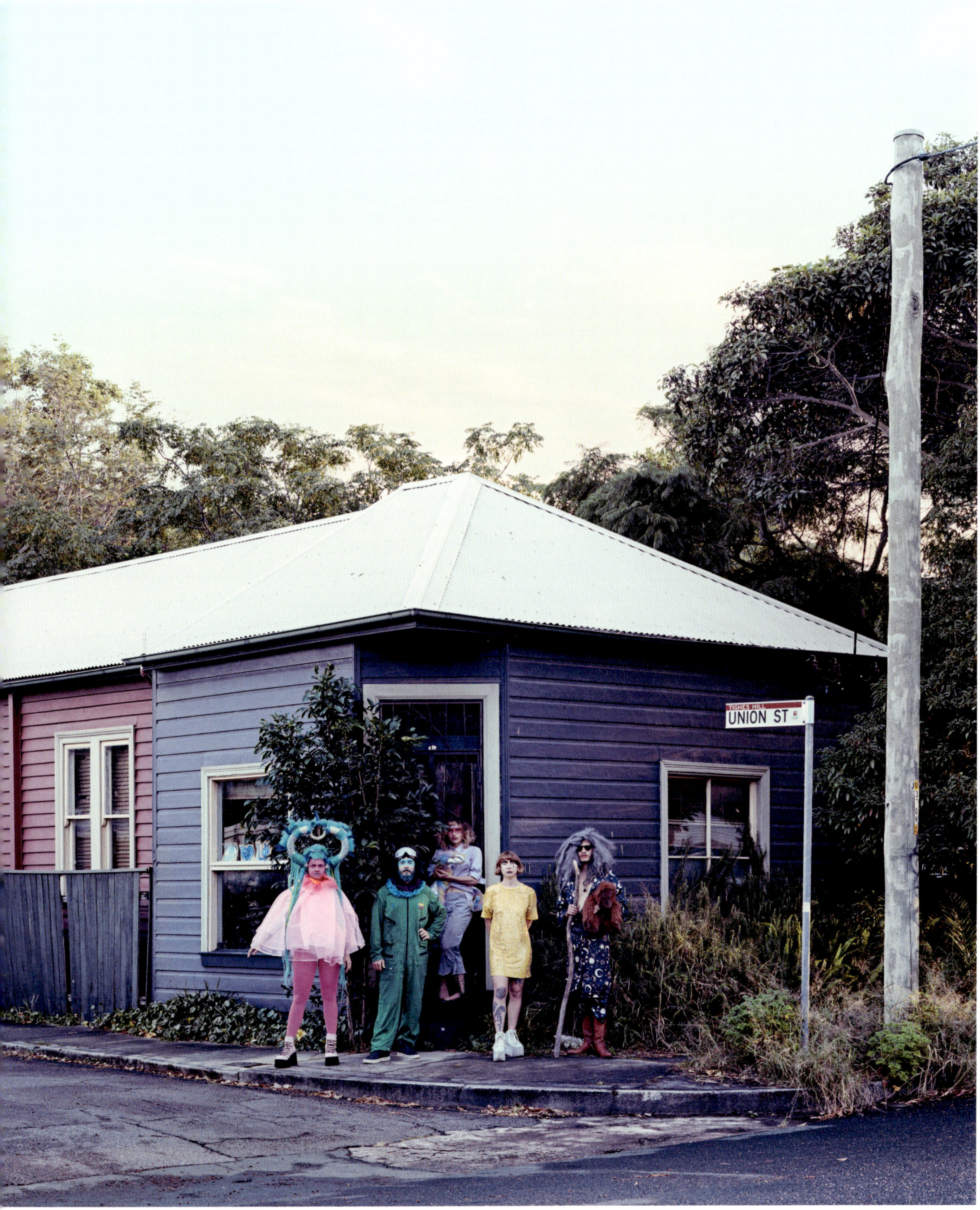
TIGHES HILL
UNION ST

Karen
3:31pm, 30 May 2020

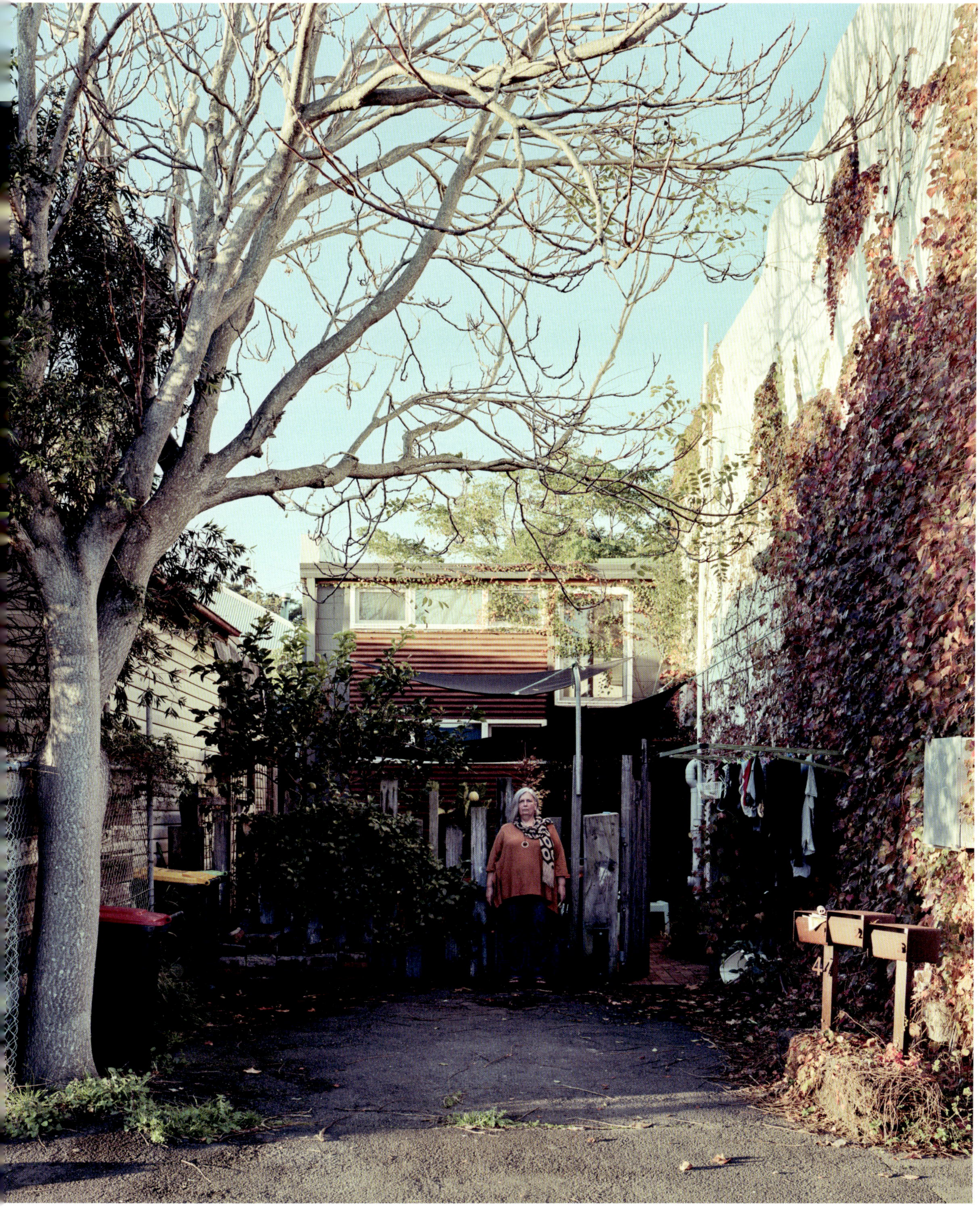

Paul and Jacklyn
4:39pm, 5 September 2021

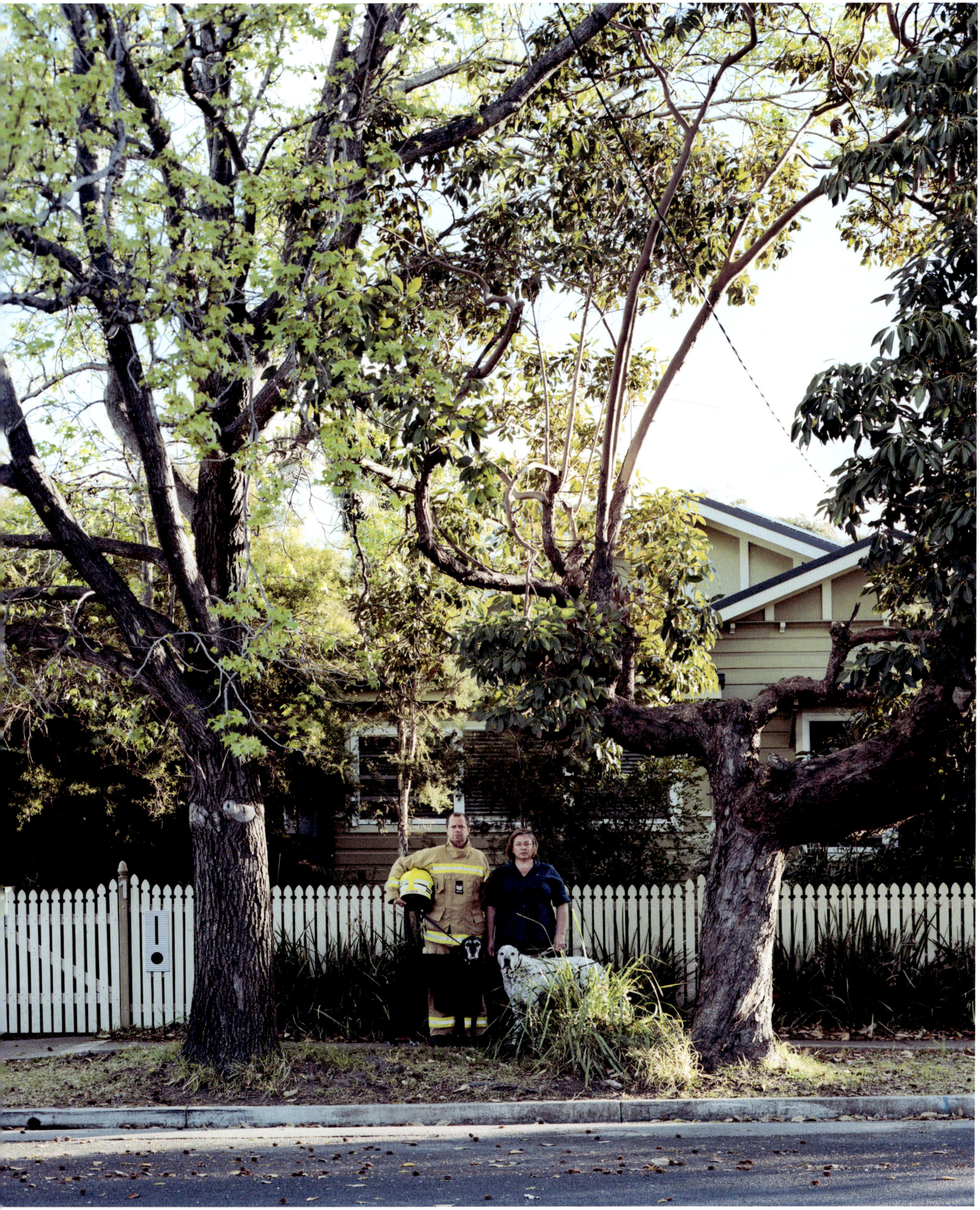

Gabriel, Laurence and Alex
4:50pm, 10 September 2021

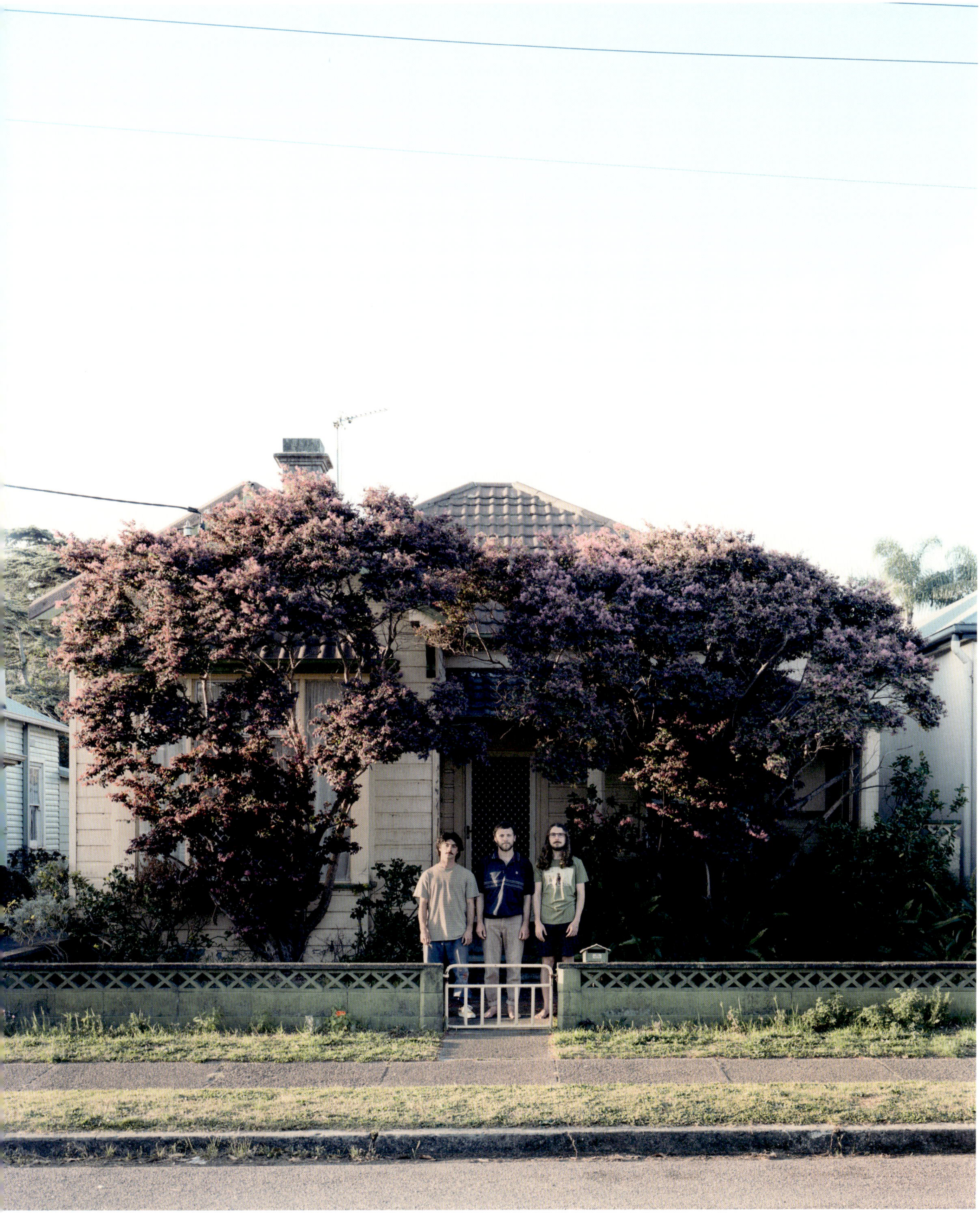

Mary
4:08pm, 21 May 2020

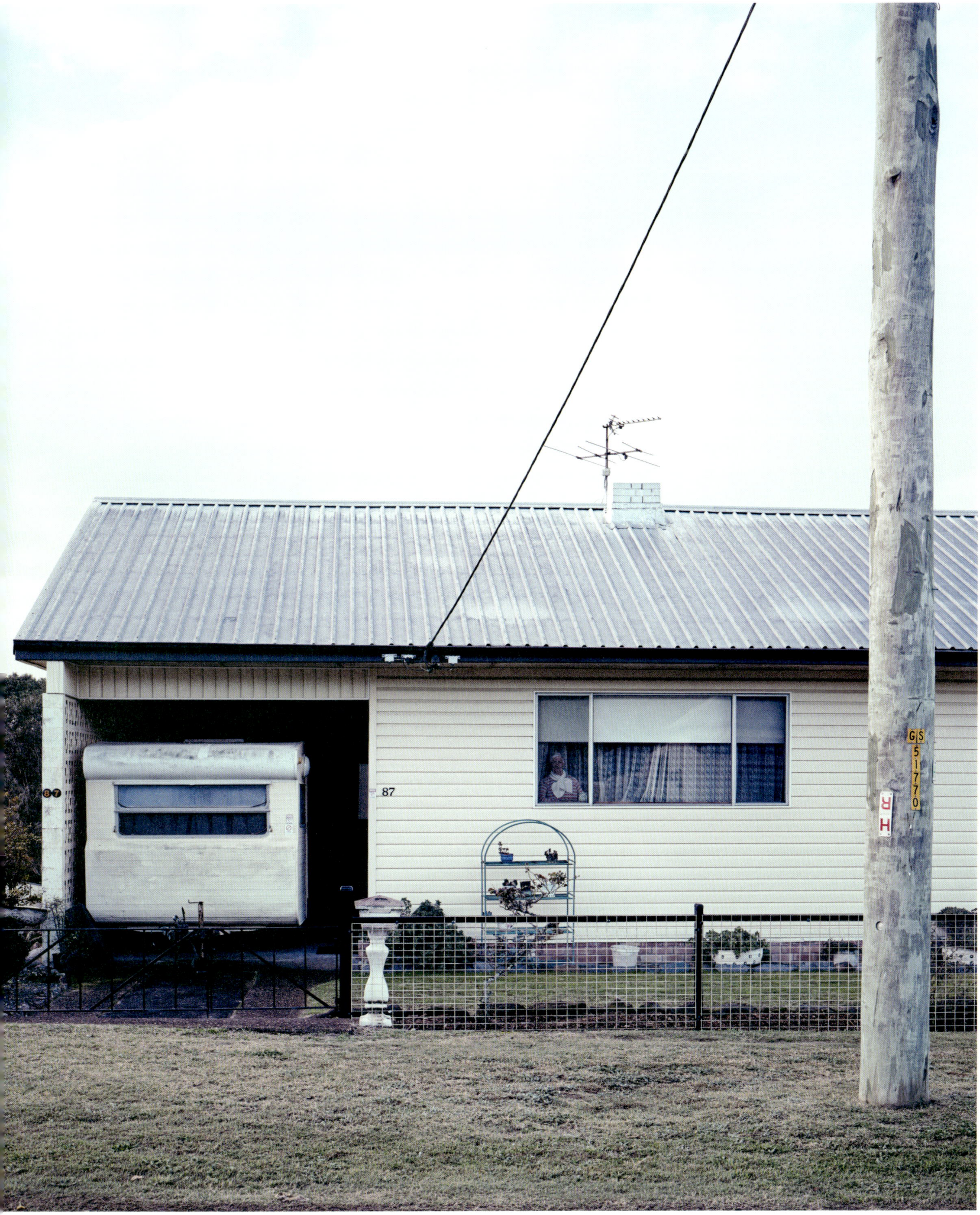
87
87
GS
51770

3 Bob, age 80, isolates on his own during the COVID-19 lockdown in Warners Bay, Australia.

5 Artists and activists, Bonnie, age 32, Ren, age 31 and Ellie, age 32, Mayfield East, Australia. An indigenous civil rights sign is displayed in their window that reads 'Land rights not mining rights.'

7 RAAF veteran, Mel, age 43, son, Henry, age 12 and daughter, Floss, age 10, in a halfway house after escaping domestic violence, Suburb undisclosed, Australia.

8 Executive creative director, Mike, age 70, partner, Liz, age 74, son and audio engineer, Rob, age 37 and daughter, Sarah, age 39, with the family dogs, Spencer and Timmy, Redhead, Australia. Mike's work has remained busy producing important health advertising during COVID-19 for his clients.

9 Medical registrar, Lauren, age 38, aerospace engineer, Greg, age 40, Lauchlan, age 6 and Chloe, age 3, Waratah, Australia. Lauren has been working as one of the COVID-19 doctors on the team in the John Hunter Hospital's intensive care unit.

11 Artists and designers, Juliana, age 39, Ben, age 43 and their daughter, Eddy, age 4, The Hill, Australia. Eddy is dressed up in a homemade robot costume she made during lockdown.

13 Newcastle University art gallery director, Gillean, in their 60s, Kent, in their 60s and Julia, in their 30s, Cooks Hill, Australia. Their son (and brother), Jambo, in his 30s, is currently in isolation in Queensland.

15 Firefighter, Peter, age 43, wife and executive officer, Sally, age 42 and children, Ace, age 6 and Frankie, age 3, New Lambton, Australia. Peter's work has remained constant being a frontline worker.

19 Communications officer, Rod, age 49, Centrelink employee, Tanya, age 43, Cooper, age 8, Jackson, age 6 and Maddie, age 4, Fletcher, Australia.

20 Gallery owners, Lisa Who, age 53 and husband, Wayne, age 52, in the flat above their gallery, Newcastle East, Australia. They have converted the front window area into a mini gallery for those walking past.

21 Artists, designers and sisters, Rowena, age 42 and Angela, age 37, at their currently-closed clothing shop, Cooks Hill, Australia.

23 Lecturer, Kevin Coffey, age 64, renowned seamstress and wife of forty years, Jean Bas Coffey, with their daughter's dog in front of their shop, Cooks Hill, Australia.

25 Paralympian, Luke Bailey, age 24, girlfriend, Megan Northey, age 24 and her son, Bryan Northey (not pictured), age 1, Wickham, Australia. Earlier in 2021 Luke competed in the Paralympic Games in Japan, representing Australia.

27 Photographer, Simone Rosenbauer, age 44, partner and design lecturer, Ralph Kenke, age 45 and son, Tino age 4, Cooks Hill, Australia.

29 Photographer, Alex, age 38, social worker, Alex, Ari, age 5, Coan, age 3 and Eli, 8-months old, Mayfield, Australia.

31 Grandmother of three, Tracey McCloy, age 63, Bar Beach, Australia.

33 Retired school teacher Carole Kaczor, age 74, husband and retired group buyer for Lowes, Stan Kaczor, Beau Vista, Merewether, Australia.

35 Abbey, age 21, has been isolating alone in her van overlooking the beach, Newcastle East, Australia.

36 Marketing coordinator, Dom Punch, age 33, his partner and nurse, Ellie, age 29, Stockton, Australia. Ellie (not pictured) is asleep after a night shift.

37 Clinical nurse, Evan O'Reilly, age 32, wife, Hannah, age 31 and their children, Fletcher, Australia. Hannah is currently studying whilst working two jobs and Evan is full time at the hospital working directly on the Respiratory and Infectious Diseases (COVID-19) ward.

39 Bartender, Tyler Visser, age 23, law student, Luisa Amosa, age 22, barista, Chloe Williams, age 23, apprentice electrician, Eli Buchanan, age 24, bartender, Orchid Knight, age 20, barista, Aidan Brady, age 21 and hospitality worker, Jordan, age 21, Maryville, Australia.

41 Real Estate business owners, Roland, age 42 and Dave, age 44, with their dog Stella, Georgetown, Australia.

42 Early childhood educator, Katherine, age 33, husband Jonathon, age 33, Cecilia, age 4 and Maria, 6-months old, Cardiff, Australia.

45 Filmmaker, Andy, age 32, wife and communications officer, Emily, age 31 and their son, River, age 2, Eleebana, Australia. Andy has continued to work in the creative industries during the pandemic, delivering important COVID-19 health videos for his clients.

46 Glazier, Alex, age 30 and student, Wednesday, age 27, Mayfield, Australia.

47 Newcastle city councillor, Carol Duncan, age 55, with family, Peter Ireland, age 46 and son, Alexander Ireland, age 19, Hamilton, Australia.

48 Festival organisers, Stephen Halpin, age 55, Wendy Gunthorpe, age 54 and housemate and psychologist, Gisela Tonal, age 63, The Hill, Newcastle, Australia.

49 Artist and designer, Trevor Dickinson, age 59 and wife, speech pathologist and lecturer, Jo Steel, age 58, New Lambton, Australia.

50 Aunty Theresa Dargin, age 41, husband, David, age 42 and family members DJ, age 21, Lauchlan, age 20, Max, age 19, Tiara, age 17, Samuel, age 15, Preston, age 10, Logan, age 10 and Sara, 10-weeks-old, New Lambton, Australia.

51 University student recruitment officer, Ray, age 39, sales rep, Kimberly, Aliah, age 14, Alyssa, age 9 and Amiia, age 5, Cameron Park, Australia.

53 Government official, Forugh Dorani, age 38, wife age 33, daughters, ages 6 and 5 and son, age 3, Chisholm, Australia. Originally from Syria, it has bee a particularly hard year for their family and friends with the ongoing conflict, on top of the pandemic.

55 Imam Mohamed A. Hamed, age 39, Mayfield Mosque, NSW, Australia. He has been separated from his wife and three children since the onset of the pandemic, as they are unable to return home from Egypt due to Australian regulations. He has been continuing to support and communicate with his community through daily online broadcasting and answering their questions via email.

57 Sophie, age 28, Aaron, age 34, Reuben, age 2 and Sidney, 3-months old, Cooks Hill, Australia.

59 Clinic coordinator, Jess Hartwig, age 34, partne Wayne, age 34 and children, Tyrone, age 19, Kayder age 13 and Makaylah, age 9, Macquarie Hills, Australia. Jess, Wayne and Tyrone are all essential workers in the medical and transport industries.

61 Professor and illustrator, Mario, age 49, artist and illustrator, Liz, age 56, their niece, Victoria, age 26 and her boyfriend Curtis, age 26, Hamilton North Australia. Victoria and Curtis recently moved to Australia for a twelve month working holiday just before the lockdown occurred. Mario's family in both Italy and the UK have been heavily impacted by COVID-19, including the recent death of his father.

63 Director/cinematographer, Thomas Hudson, age 36, university worker and wife, Laura Hudson, age 37 and daughter, Eden, age 2, Tighes Hill, Australia.

5 Chef, Jordan, age 24, student, Keelan, age 24, afe manager, Charlee, age 19, nanny, Rhian, age 21 nd student, Liam, age 25, Cooks Hill, Australia.

7 Audience development coordinator at the ewcastle Art Gallery, Zana, age 30 and partner, atrick, age 33, with their puppy Miro, isolate in the djoining house to her mum, Karen, age 58, lington, Australia.

8 Communications officer, Chelsey age 38, esigner, Chris, age 38, Izzy, age 9 and Lara, age , with the family guinea pigs, Mayfield, Australia.

9 Art gallery director, Courtney, age 41, Adam, ge 42, Oli, age 12, Charlie, age 9, Francesca, age and their dogs, Basil and Stevie, Newcastle East, ustralia.

Bus driver, Kieran, age 34, partner and bank fficer, Renae, age 40, daughter, Iris age 2 and eir rescued greyhound, Esther, Belmont, Australia. ieran and Renae's work has remained busy as they e classed as essential workers.

3 Startup founder and CEO, Jacqui, age 39, usband and retail manager, Ben, age 40, son, Max, ge 12 and mum, Helen, age 71, Belmont North, ustralia. Jacqui was about to receive a life nanging amount of seed funding for her startup usiness just before COVID-19 and is currently orking around the clock to try and secure new nding opportunities.

5 Police chief inspector, David Matthews, age 8, wife, Tamara, age 47 and children, Lily, age 11 nd Flynn age 7, Valentine, Australia. When the nset of the Delta variant entered Australia, avid led the Pandemic Operations team for ake Macquarie Police District.

7 Photographer, Max Mason-Hubers, age 33, hD candidate (clinical epidemiology and public ealth) and partner, Heather Valerio, age 32, The ill, Newcastle, Australia.

9 Greg, age 56, Newcastle CBD, Australia. Greg, ho is currently unhoused, takes shelter in a public oilet block with his belongings.

1 Newcastle's lord mayor, Nuatali Nelmes, age 45, usband and manager of industrial maintenance tes, Stuart Nelmes and their children, Archie, tella-Rose and Ruby-Lou, all students, Merewether, ustralia. Nautili's role has seen a significant crease in her media and communication duties nce the pandemic began.

82 Artists, Marigold, age 32 and Zack, age 45, in front of their art warehouse where they work from each day, Maryville, Australia.

83 Tourism worker, Alex Morris, age 34, partner and TAFE teacher, Josh Bruce, age 40, Newcastle West, Australia.

85 Vet, Simon Lubans, age 49 and his dog Whoppet, Cooks Hill, Newcastle, New South Wales, Australia. As an essential worker, he has continued to help his patients throughout lockdown.

87 Musician, Mia, age 23, masseur, Phoebe, age 24, artist, Ramona, age 23, support worker Liam, age 25, communications student, Tegan and psychology student, Kirra, Broadmeadow, Australia.

88 Artist, Catherine, age 63, Newcastle East, Australia.

89 Broadcast designer, Helen, age 34 and final year speech pathology student, Bridget, age 31, Newcastle East, Australia.

91 Leatherworker and shop owner, Geordie, age 33, vintage clothing collector and shop owner, Eartha, age 42, daughter, Emmylou, age 6 and son, Howlin, age 12, Georgetown, Australia.

93 Artists, Jeptha, Tegan, Kristen, Jerry and Genevieve, dress up in handmade costumes, Tighes Hill, Australia.

95 Lawyer, Karen, age 58, isolates in the adjoining house to her daughter, Zana, age 30, Islington, Australia. Karen has been working throughout the pandemic having to dial into court cases via video to support her clients.

97 Fireman, Paul Burke, age 51, nurse, Jacklyn Burke, age 42 and their two dogs, Arty and Indie, Mayfield West, Australia. Being first responders, they have continued to work since the lockdowns began in 2020.

99 Graduate engineer, Gabriel Zalcman, age 27, student Laurence Gracia-Villada, age 27 and graduate engineer, Alex Fairclough, age 27, Hamilton, Australia.

101 Retired factory worker, Mary, age 81, next to her unused caravan, Abermaine, Australia.

As a photographer, I have always been fascinated by the human condition and have spent my career documenting people through photographs. In 2020, the world was plunged into a global pandemic, which changed the human experience in ways we could not have predicted.

When the first COVID-19 public health lockdowns and closures were announced, I wondered what this would mean for my local community in Newcastle, NSW. Australia had some of the strictest stay-at-home lockdowns in the world, initially in 2020 and then a second hard lockdown occurring in late 2021. I felt compelled to photograph the experience and contribute to a collective memory of this historical moment.

The resulting project is a series of 100 portraits from different households in isolation. Each household experience was recorded through written interviews and photographed in a typographical style on 4x5 large format film. I chose this format to create a structure and rigidity to the images as well as creating distortion free photographs of built-environments, allowing the viewer to focus on the individuals and not be distracted by a changing composition.

Because of the lockdowns, I developed all of the colour sheet film myself. Developing large format colour film by hand is a complex process that inevitably leads to unexpected results and technical flaws in the images. Instead of working to remove these, I embraced them to help express some of the surreal experiences we all shared together.

Through the interviews accompanying each photograph, the project documents the thoughts, fears, and hopes for the future of each household, providing a glimpse into the human experience during a time of uncertainty and isolation. My hope is that the project will stimulate a deeper reflection on our shared humanity in years to come and serve as a reminder of our ability to come together in times of crisis.

Luke David Kellett

Thank yous
To my family: my wife Sarah, son Jude, mum Clare, dad Joe, grandad Geoff, grandma Mary, brother Mike, sister-in-laws Laura and Rachel, mother-in-law Cindy and partner Nick, nephew Jack, aunties Dee, Helen, Julia, Jo and Rosie, uncles Brian, David, Steve, Tony and all my cousins.

To my mentors: George Ktistakis, Lee Williams and all at Rapid Eye London, James Geer, Mike Preston, Julie Baird and Mark Power.

To the whole Headjam team—past, present and future and to my friends Ebony, Tanja, Lumi, Camille, Mary, Sasha, Lenny, Simone, Ralph and Tino.
A huge thank you.

Notes
The work was first exhibited in late 2020 at the Newcastle Museum, curated by Director Julie Baird. In 2021, the State Library of New South Wales acquired this body of work and it now forms part of their permanent collection for future generations to access.

Newcastle
First published in 2023
by GOST Books, London

info@gostbooks.com
gostbooks.com

Edited and designed by GOST:
Rossella Castello, Katie Clifford,
Gemma Gerhard, Justine Hucker,
Allon Kaye, Eleanor Macnair,
Claudia Paladini, Ana Rocha

Printed in Italy by EBS

British Library cataloguing-in publication data.
A catalogue record of this book is available from the British Library.

ISBN 978-1-910401-99-6